D0605029

PETER DECHANT
Box 415
MANNING, ALBERTA

GREYSTONE'S

Creative Hands

EDITOR

Beverley Hilton

GREYSTONE PRESS/NEW YORK · TORONTO · LONDON

Volume 3

Contents

© Fratelli Fabri Editore, Milan 1966, 1967
Marshall Cavendish Limited 1970, 1971, 1972, 1973, 1975
Manufactured in the United States of America
Library of Congress Catalog Card No. 75-8338

Much of the material contained herein has
previously been published in separate parts
under the title Golden Hands.

Collector's Piece

Danish rose	290
The Age of Treasured Books	320

Crochet: Basic Wardrobe

Prettiest suit in town (part 1)	284
Prettiest suit in town (part 2)	304

Crochet Know-how

Fair and square	226
Designing with motifs	246
Fancy trimmings	266
Lace and flower star motifs	283
Place mats and tray cloths	306
Narcissi and daisies	326

Dressmaking

Focus on hems and belts	236
Prepare to pleat	256
One pattern – many skirts	276
Knife-pleated skirt	294
The basic blouse	316

Embroidery

Cross-stitch methods	228
The feather stitch family	250
Tambour work on caftans	268
Enlarging and reducing designs	284
The art of appliqué	308
Designing for appliqué	328

Embroidery on Tulle

Enmeshed stitches	292

Fashion Flair

Butterflies, chickens and ducklings	240
Coutry style embroidery	260
Sleeping pretty	280
Add to dressmaking with knitting	330

Home Sewing

Collector's pillows	288

Knitting: Basic Wardrobe

Knit two dresses from one pattern	224
A pretty useful pullover	264
Snowsuits	324

Knitting Know-how

Picking up stitches and weaving	222
Lacy look stitches	242
Specially for 12-year-olds	262
Rose-embroidered baby bootees	282
Double crossed stitches	302
Doll's party dress and coat	322

Machine Knitting: Basic Wardrobe

Racy, lacy party looks	244

Needlepoint

Crisscross stitches	232
Satin smooth	252
Apple pin cushion	272
A bold and beautiful bolero	310

Netting

Basic netting	314

Pattern Library

Daisy alphabet	221
Basketful of posies	241
Jacquard stitch	261
Strawberries and toadstools	281
Appliqué flower	301

Take Care

All about fabrics and fibers	297

Tatting

Lovely lace that's easy to make	234
Double knots and picots	254

Toy Making

Lamb	274

Pattern Library

Daisy alphabet

Instructions for the second half of the alphabet initials, in lazy daisy stitch, are the same as those given in the last Pattern Library chapter, page 201.

Picking up stitches and weaving

The yarn color and texture you've chosen are perfect, the needles are right, the gauge is correct and all your knitted pieces look immaculate. If you're asking yourself, "now what?" the answer is that still more care is required. The finishing stages must be done well if your garment is to look really professional. Knitted borders, collars, cuffs or contrasting edgings, for example, can be ruined if stitched on by hand with thick, lumpy seams which are impossible to press. Picking up stitches instead is really a very simple job if it's done methodically, but it can completely mar the finished effect if it is worked carelessly or without very cautious regard for regularity.

Weaving, also, is often overlooked as a method of finishing. The directions on these pages give weaving for stockinette stitch (which is used most frequently) and also for joining purl fabrics, garter stitch and ribbing.

Picking up stitches

This method of finishing a neckline or other edge will save you the trouble of casting on a separate collar, cuff, or edging and sewing it on when completing the garment. Picking up stitches is not difficult, but you must be sure to work very carefully if you want to save time and avoid disappointment.

It is usual to begin to pick up stitches with the right side of the work facing you. The directions will always specify if this is not the case in a particular pattern.

Lifting stitches onto the needle with a crochet hook

Lifting stitches with an afghan hook—very practical for this purpose

The most widely known method involves using the same knitting needle which you will use to knit the edging. Hold the yarn behind the work and insert the tip of the needle through the stitch, drawing through a loop of yarn to the right side and forming one loop on the needle. Continue until all the required stitches are on the needle.

Some knitters prefer to draw the loop of yarn through with a crochet hook, then slip the loop onto the needle to be used. There is, however, a tool on the market which makes the entire process much easier. It is an afghan hook, which looks like a long slender knitting needle with a hook on one end. The hook end is used just as the crochet hook to draw the loop through. It is then on the needle and does not need to be transferred to another one. Once the stitches have been picked up, you can then knit them off the other end with the correct size needle.

In order to have the yarn end up already attached at the pointed end for knitting, measure in from the end of the ball about three times the length of the row to be picked up and then work from this point back toward the end as you pick up the loops. If you don't feel you can judge the length required, then use a separate length of yarn for picking up the stitches and join in the ball of yarn in the normal way when you begin to knit the stitches on to the correct size needle.

You will only need a fine size afghan hook. The thinness of this size is a great help in drawing loops through firmer fabrics and there is no chance of the loop slipping off and staying on the wrong side as happens only too often when using a knitting needle. If you are picking up stitches around a neck, or on a long edge, it is always easier to mark the edge into sections than to use the trial and error method. Some directions will give you detailed information as to exactly how many stitches should be on the back neck, side neck and the center front of the neck; but sooner or later you will be confronted with a pattern which states that you have to pick up 124 stitches evenly around the neck. If you always make it a practice to divide the edge by putting in marker pins, then you will have no trouble and will not have to try again and again to get the correct number of stitches. Mark the center back and front with pins, then fold this in half again and insert two more pins. Now you will know that between pins you have a quarter of the total number of stitches to pick up. If you treat every edge in this way, dividing it as often as you like, it is easy to pick up the correct number of stitches at once.

Weaving

Weaving is a method of joining two rows of stitches invisibly. It is used in knitting mittens and at the toes of socks where the ridge formed by a seamed bound-off edge would be uncomfortable. It is also most useful for joining buttonhole and button strips where they are not continuous but meet at the center back of the neck. The bulkiness of underarm seams can be completely avoided by leaving the stitches normally bound off at armholes and sleeve cap shapings unworked and by weaving them together before the remainder of the sleeve and side seams are worked. Weaving is usually worked on stockinette, purled or garter stitch surfaces, but, if worked with care, can also be used for joining ribbing.

Weaving off needles

When the edges are ready for weaving, cut off the ball of yarn, leaving an end about three to four times the length of the row to be woven, and thread this into a darning needle. The illustrations below show a contrast colored yarn being threaded through the stitches so that you can see it clearly. As the weave is to be invisible, you would naturally use the same yarn as the garment. The illustrations also show the stitches slipped off the needles. Some knitters do weave in this way, but there is always the danger of dropping one or more of the stitches.

Weaving on needles

To weave two stockinette stitch edges together, have the stitches on two knitting needles, one behind the other, length of yarn threaded into the darning needle and needle points, all at the right-hand side of the work with the wrong sides of work touching.
Insert the threaded darning needle into the first stitch on the front

knitting needle as if to purl it and draw the yarn through, leaving the stitch on the knitting needle. *Insert the darning needle into the first stitch on the back knitting needle as if to purl it and slip it off the knitting needle, then insert the darning needle into the next stitch on the back needle as if to knit it and leave it on the knitting needle, but draw the yarn through. Insert the darning needle into the first stitch on the front knitting needle as if to knit it and slip it off the knitting needle, then insert the darning needle into the next stitch on the front needle as if to purl it, leaving it on the knitting needle, but pulling the yarn through. Now repeat from * until all the stitches have been worked off. When you draw the yarn through, don't pull it too tight or leave it too slack. The row of weaving stitches should be the same size as the knitted ones, thus making them invisible. If they are not even, use the darning needle to work the yarn along the row before finishing off the end, pulling wide stitches smaller or working extra yarn along the row if the stitches are too tight. When you are weaving hold the needles with the stitches on them in your left hand, keeping the stitches near the tips of the needles so that you do not need to tug at them to slip them off the points.

To weave two edges of purl fabric together, work in the same way as for stockinette stitch, reading knit for purl and purl for knit. It is, however, possible to turn the knitting to the wrong side and work as for stockinette stitch, turning to the right side when the weaving is finished.

To weave ribbed edges together, just learn both of the above methods. If you do this, you will then be able to weave any type of ribbed edges together because you simply use both methods in combination. In other words, you will join stockinette stitch rib to stockinette stitch rib with the stockinette stitch method, and join purl rib to purl rib using the purl method.

▲ *Weaving stockinette stitch, knit side facing (contrast yarn only for clarity)*
▼ *Weaving stockinette stitch with purl side facing is worked similarly*

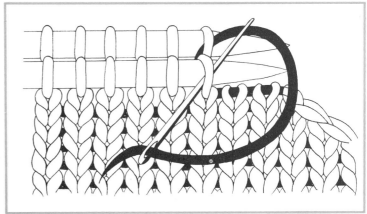

Weaving stockinette stitch on needles which are held in the left hand

To weave garter stitch edges, you work as given for stockinette stitch, but you must first make certain that the last row knitted on the front needle left a ridge on the right side of the work and that the last row on the back needle formed a ridge on the wrong side or inside of the work. It may be necessary to add or take off a row on either side to obtain this before beginning to weave.
Weaving may seem involved the first time, but it is not difficult and there is one easy way to work it out. The yarn passes through each stitch twice. The first time it enters the stitch, it enters in the opposite way to the type of stitch. That is, into a knit stitch you must insert the needle purlwise and into a purl stitch you must insert the needle knitwise—the stitch is left on the knitting needle. The second time the stitch is slipped off the knitting needle after the darning needle has passed through it for the same type of stitch. This means that the second time you pass the darning needle knitwise into a knit stitch and purlwise into a purl stitch.

Knit two from one pattern

A simply sculptured dress with side ribbed panels always looks lovely. The sleeveless version can be worn either as a jumper, or as a stunning party dress with beads, a belt or a scarf.

Sizes

Directions are for 32in bust with 34in hips.
Length down center back, 35½ [35¾:36:36¼]in.
Sleeve seam, 17 [17:17½:18]in. The figures in brackets [ ] refer to the 34, 36 and 38in bust with 36, 38, and 40in hip sizes respectively.

Gauge for this design
6sts and 8 rows to 1 inch measured over stockinette stitch worked on No.3 needles

Materials

Columbia-Minerva Linspun, 2 oz. balls
Long-sleeved dress:
8 [8:9:9] balls
Sleeveless dress:
6 [6:6:7] balls
One pair No.2 needles or Canadian No. 11
One pair No.3 needles or Canadian No. 10
One belt buckle

Long-sleeved dress back

Using No.3 needles, cast on 135 [141:147:153] sts.
Beg with a K row, work 8 rows in st st.
Change to No.2 needles and work 3 rows more in st st.
Hemline row K all stitches.
Beg with a K row, work 3 rows in st st.

Basic Wardrobe Knitting

Change to No.3 needles and continue in st st.
Work 12 rows more.
1st dec row K2, K2 tog, K38 [40:42:44], K2 tog tbl, K1, K2 tog, K41 [43:45:47], K2 tog tbl, K1, K2 tog, K38 [40:42:44], K2 tog tbl, K2.
Work 25 rows.
2nd dec row K2, K2 tog, K36 [38:40:42], K2 tog tbl, K1, K2 tog, K39 [41:43:45], K2 tog tbl, K1, K2 tog, K36 [38:40:42], K2 tog tbl, K2.
Work 25 rows.
Dec 6sts in this way on next and following 26th row.
111 [117:123:129] sts.
Work one row.

Begin side ribbed panels
1st row P3, K3, P3, K to last 9sts, P3, K3, P3.
2nd row K3, P3, K3, P to last 9sts, K3, P3, K3.
Rep last 2 rows 4 times more.
11th row P3, (K3, P3) twice, K to last 15sts, (P3, K3) twice, P3.
12th row K3, (P3, K3) twice, P to last 15sts, (K3, P3) twice, K3.
Rep last 2 rows 4 times more. Continue in this way, working 6sts more at either side into rib patt on next and every 10th row until there are 39sts in side panels.
Work 42 rows, keeping rib and st st as established.
Next row Rib 33, K to last 33sts, rib 33.
Work 9 rows.
Next row Rib 27, K to last 27sts, rib 27.
Continue to work 6sts less in rib on either side of every 10th row until the work measures 28in (or desired length) from hemline to underarm, ending

with a WS row.
While shaping the armholes, continue to work ribbing as before, until there are no rib sts remaining.

Shape armholes
Bind off 6 [7:8:9] sts at beg of next 2 rows.
Bind off 3sts at beg of next 2 rows.
Bind off 2sts at beg of next 4 rows.
Bind off 1 st at beg of next 4 rows.
Work 44 [46:48:50] rows without shaping.

Shape shoulders and neck
Bind off 4 [5:6:7] sts at beg of next 2 rows.
Bind off 5sts at beg of next 2 rows.
5th row Bind off 5sts, K 17, bind off center 19 [21:23:25], K to end.
Complete left shoulder on these sts.
6th row Bind off 5sts, P to end.
7th row Bind off 7sts, K to end.
8th row Bind off 5sts, P to end.
9th row K.
10th row Bind off rem 5sts.
With WS work facing, attach yarn to rem sts.
Next row Bind off 7sts, P to end.
Next row Bind off 5sts, K to end.
Next row P.
Next row Bind off rem 5sts.

Front

Work as given for back until 29 [31:33:35] rows have been worked after completion of armhole shaping.

Shape neck
1st row K34 [35:36:37], bind off 13 [15:17:19], K to end.
** Complete right shoulder on these sts.
Bind off at beg of RS rows 3sts once, 2sts twice and 1 st 3 times. 24 [25:26:27] sts.
Work 2 rows.

Shape shoulder
Bind off at armhole edge on next and every other row 4 [5:6:7] sts once and 5sts 4 times.**
With WS of work facing, attach

yarn to rem sts and work left shoulder as for right from ** to **, binding off for neck shaping on WS rows.

Sleeves

With No.2 needles, cast on 55 [55:61:61] sts.
1st row K2, P3, *K3, P3, rep from * to last 2sts, K2.
2nd row P2, K3, *P3, K3, rep from * to last 2sts, P2.
Rep 1st and 2nd rows 9 times more, inc one st at each end of last row.
Change to No.3 needles.
Continue in K3, P3 rib throughout, working inc sts into patt as they are made.
Work 6 rows.
Inc one st at each end of next and every 6th row until there are 85 [89:93:97] sts.
Work until sleeve measures 17 [17:17½:18] in, or desired length, ending with a WS row.

Shape cap
Bind off 6 [7:8:9] sts at beg of next 2 rows.
Bind off 3sts at beg of next 2 rows.
Bind off 2sts at beg of next 2 rows.
Dec one st at each end of next and every other row until 41sts rem, then every row until 31sts rem.
K3 tog at each end of next 6 rows. Bind off.

Belt

With No.2 needles, cast on 18sts. Work in K2, P2 rib until 30in long.
Dec one st at each end of every row until 4sts rem.
Bind off.

Neckband

Join right shoulder seam.
With No.2 needles and RS work facing, pick up and K 102 [108:114:120] sts.
Work 7 rows K3, P3 rib.
Bind off in rib.

Finishing

PRESS LIGHTLY UNDER A DAMP CLOTH WITH A WARM IRON

Join all seams and neckband. Sew in sleeves. Sew buckle to straight edge of belt.

Sleeveless dress back

Work as given for long-sleeved dress back.

Front

Work as for back until armhole shaping has been completed. Work 15 [17:19:21] rows without shaping.

Shape neck
1st row K34 [35:36:37], bind off 13 [15:17:19] sts, K to end. Complete right shoulder on these sts.
** Bind off on RS rows 3sts. once, 2sts twice and 1 st 3 times.
Work 14 rows.

Shape shoulder
Work as given for long-sleeved dress front.**
With WS facing, attach yarn to rem sts. Work as for other shoulder from ** to ** binding off for neck shaping on WS rows.

Neckband

Join right shoulder seam. With No.2 needles, RS facing, pick up and K132 [138:144:150] sts evenly around neck edge. Work 7 rows K3, P3 rib. Bind off in rib. Join left shoulder seam and neckband.

Armbands

With No.2 needles, RS facing, pick up and K120 [126:132:138] sts evenly around armhole. Work 3 rows K3, P3 rib. Bind off in rib.

Finishing

Finish as directed for long-sleeved dress. Sew side and armband seams.

The two versions of the dress ▶

Fair and square

As you probably realize by now, motifs have endless uses, not only for pillow cases and afghans, but also for a variety of fashion ideas. You've already seen how easy it is to make a vest (chapter 6, page 106)—in future chapters you'll see how simple it is to put together other wardrobe items (a blouse is next). In the meantime, here are two new motifs to try.

Colors and yarns

Try out several color ideas until you find something you particularly like. It could be a collection of gay chunky wools worked with a large hook so that the motifs grow quickly and are then joined (see Crochet Know-how, chapter 5, page 86) to form a long scarf. Or trim the lower edges and sleeves of an evening blouse with a row of motifs worked in a fine metallic yarn. Just remember that if you are using only one color you do not need to break the yarn, but simply continue with the next round, omitting the slip stitch used to join in a new color.

Directions are given for the same color combinations as those shown in the illustrations. Try using your own choice of colors and see the difference if you work in only one or two. Or work with the darkest color in the center and graduate out to the pale one.

Square motif

With center color, ch10. Join into a circle with a ss.
1st round. Using same color, ch3 to form the first st, work 23dc into circle. Join with ss into 3rd of first 3ch. Break yarn, leaving an end to darn in later.
2nd round. Using 1st contrast, join to top of last st of preceding round with a ss, ch3 to form first st, ch5, 1dc into same st as first st, ch7, *skip 5dc of preceding round, work 1dc, ch5, 1dc all into next dc, ch7, rep from * twice. Join with ss into 3rd of first 3ch.
3rd round. Ch3 to form first st, work 4dc, ch5, 4dc all into first ch5 space of preceding round, ch3, *skip ch7 space, 5dc, ch5, 5dc all into next ch5 space, ch3, rep from * twice. Join with ss into 3rd of first 3ch. Break yarn, leaving end for darning.
4th round. Using second contrast, join as before, ch3 to form first st, 1dc into each of next 4dc of preceding round, work 3dc, ch5, 3dc all into next ch5 space, work 1dc into each of next 5dc, ch7, *1dc into each of next 5dc, work 3dc, ch5, 3dc all into next ch5 space, 1dc into each of next 5dc, ch7, rep from * twice. Join with ss into 3rd of first 3ch. Break yarn, leaving end for darning.
5th round. Join in third contrast as before, ch3 to form first st, 1dc into each of next 7dc of preceding round, 9dc into next ch5 space, 1dc into each of next 8dc, ch3, 1sc into 4th (center) ch of ch7, ch3, *1dc into each of next 8dc, 9dc into next ch5 space, 1dc into each of next 8dc, ch3, 1sc into 4th ch of ch7, ch3, rep from * twice. Join with ss into 3rd of first 3ch. Break yarn, leaving end for darning.
6th round. Join in fourth contrast as before, ch1, work 1sc into each dc or sc of preceding round, working 3sc into each ch3 space. Join with ss to first ch. Break yarn and darn in end. Be careful when doing this to darn into the same color, so that the ends are invisible and the pattern not spoiled. If you have used wool or cotton, pin out the motif to form a good, regular shape and press under a damp cloth with a warm iron. Do not press too heavily or the stitches will be flattened. Do not press man-made fibers. Sew the motifs together at points where they touch each other.

Star motif with 8 points

Using center color, ch7. Join into a circle with a ss.
1st round. Ch2 to form first st, work 23sc into circle. Join with ss to 2nd of first 2ch. Break yarn, leaving end for darning.
2nd round. Join contrast yarn with ss to top of last st worked, ch4, 1dc into same st as first st, ch1, *skip 2sc of preceding round, 1dc, ch2, 1dc all into next sc, ch1, rep from * 6 times. Join with ss into 2nd of first 4ch.
3rd round. With same color, ch2, 1dc, ch2, 2dc all into first ch2 space of preceding round, 1sc into next ch1 space, *2dc, ch2, 2dc all into next ch2 space, 1sc into next ch1 space, rep from * 6 times. Join with ss into 2nd of first 2ch. Break yarn.
4th round. Join in first color as before, ch2, 2dc, ch1, 3dc all into first ch2 space of preceding round, 1sc on each side of sc of preceding round, *3dc, ch1, 3dc all into next ch2 space, 1sc on each side of next sc, rep from * 6 times. Join with ss into 2nd of first 2ch. Break yarn, leaving end for darning.
5th round. Join in contrast as before, ch2, 1sc into each of next 3dc, 1sc, ch3, 1sc all into first ch1 space, 1sc into each of next 4dc, *1sc into each of next 4dc, 1sc, ch3, 1sc all into next ch1 space, 1sc into each of next 4dc, rep from * 6 times. Join with ss into 2nd of first 2ch. Break yarn and darn in all ends. Complete as for square motif if pressing is required.

◄ *Square motif in 4-ply sport yarn using No.H hook, 5½in across*
Star motif using the same yarn and hook as the square, 6½in across ►

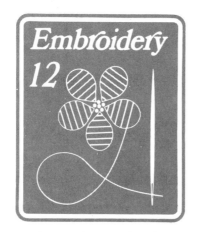

Cross-stitch methods

Cross-stitch is one of the oldest and most international embroidery stitches, frequently found in the national costumes of Europe and the Orient where it is often worked in gay, bright colors. It lends itself to fillings and building up traditional geometric patterns, as in Assisi designs, and is also used for interpreting realistic and precisely detailed pictures in the modern Danish manner. It would look equally pretty embroidered around the hem of a dress for a peasant effect.

Ideally, cross-stitch should be worked on an even-weave fabric because this makes it easier to count threads, and the whole effect of the stitch depends on its regularity. Each cross-stitch should make a perfect square, since it is worked down and across over an equal number of threads on an even-weave fabric.

The main point to remember is that in whichever direction you work the stitch, the upper stitches must always lie in the same direction (usually from bottom left to top right). If they do not, they will reflect the light differently from the other stitches and will stand out clearly as mistakes.

Methods of working

The most even finish for filling in large areas of color is obtained by working a row of diagonal stitches (half cross-stitches) in one direction and then completing the stitches by working another row in the opposite direction. If you are working an entire design in cross-stitch, keep the texture even by first working the whole design in half cross-stitch and then completing it in the other direction. This also helps you see results very rapidly. If there is only a small area to cover, it is permissible to use the method where one stitch is completed at a time, although this will look less even. To embroider very fine or uneven fabrics, use the canvas method to keep the stitches even. Place a piece of soft cotton canvas

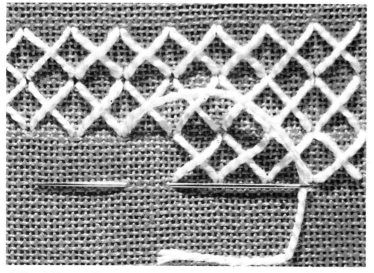

When filling small areas, complete one stitch at a time. Be careful to count the threads, using the weave of the fabric as a guide so that the stitches line up evenly. Work from either left to right or right to left.

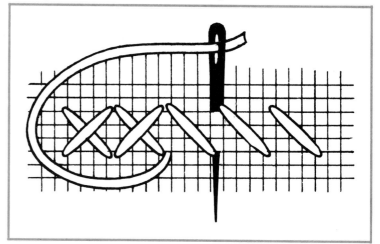

▲ *For large areas it is best to work the cross-stitch in two operations*
▼ *Double cross-stitch steps should be worked in the same order throughout*

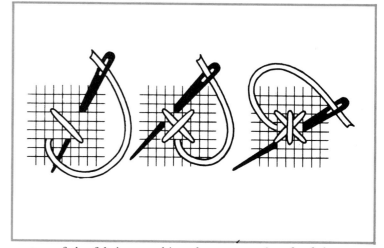

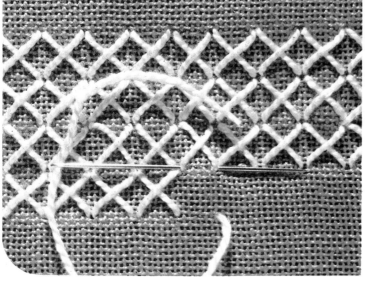

on top of the fabric, matching the warp and weft of the canvas to that of the fabric. Baste it in place. Work the stitches over the threads of the canvas and through the material underneath, being careful not to catch the canvas or pull the stitches too tight. When the embroidery is completely finished, gently pull out the canvas threads one by one.

Home is where the heart is

This gay picture brings a fresh modern approach to the old sampler idea. It was designed to be a very special birthday greeting for the designer's husband, but it could be mounted equally well on a small tray and covered with heatproof glass.

Working charts and full instructions are given on the following two pages along with color suggestions.

These charts are planned in such a way that you can either use the motifs individually, or group them to add up to the complete composition. Each motif has its own color coding, which is indicated by the key at the side of each chart. One of the best features of charted designs is that they provide a permanent reference which you can use again and again.

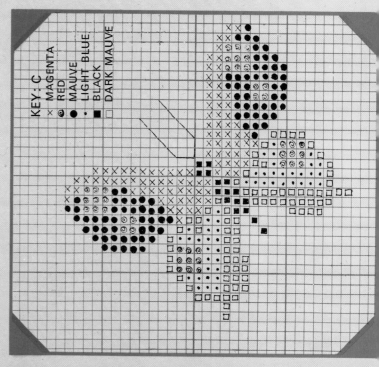

KEY: C
× MAGENTA
◉ RED
● MAUVE
• LIGHT BLUE
■ BLACK
□ DARK MAUVE

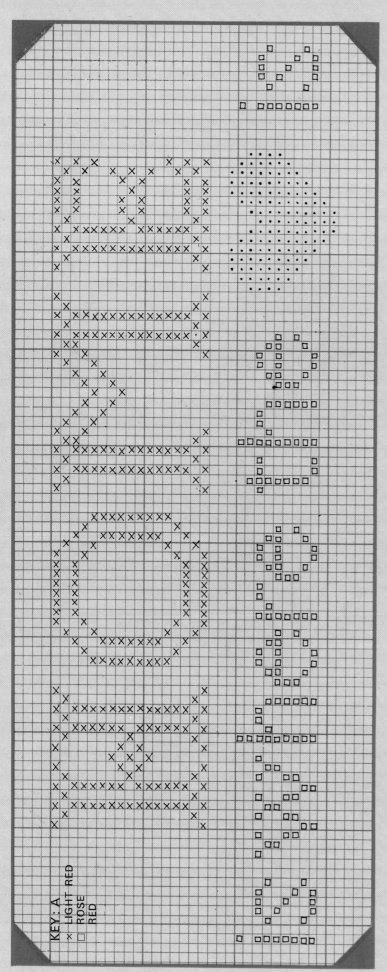

KEY: A
× LIGHT RED
□ ROSE
RED

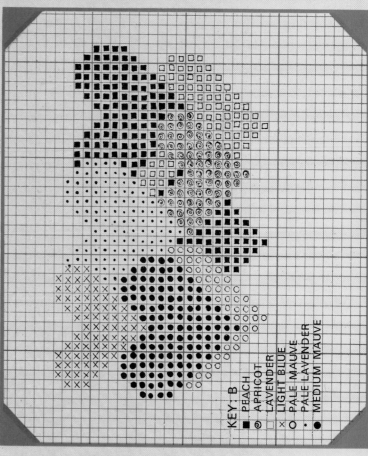

KEY: B
■ PEACH
□ APRICOT
LAVENDER
× LIGHT BLUE
○ PALE MAUVE
• PALE LAVENDER
● MEDIUM MAUVE

Materials

To make the picture shown (finished size 9in by 8½in) you will need:

☐ ⅜yd of even-weave linen (28 threads to the inch)
☐ 1 skein each of 6-strand embroidery floss in the colors given on the charts, but the leaf green needs 2 skeins
☐ Crewel needle size 8 or 9

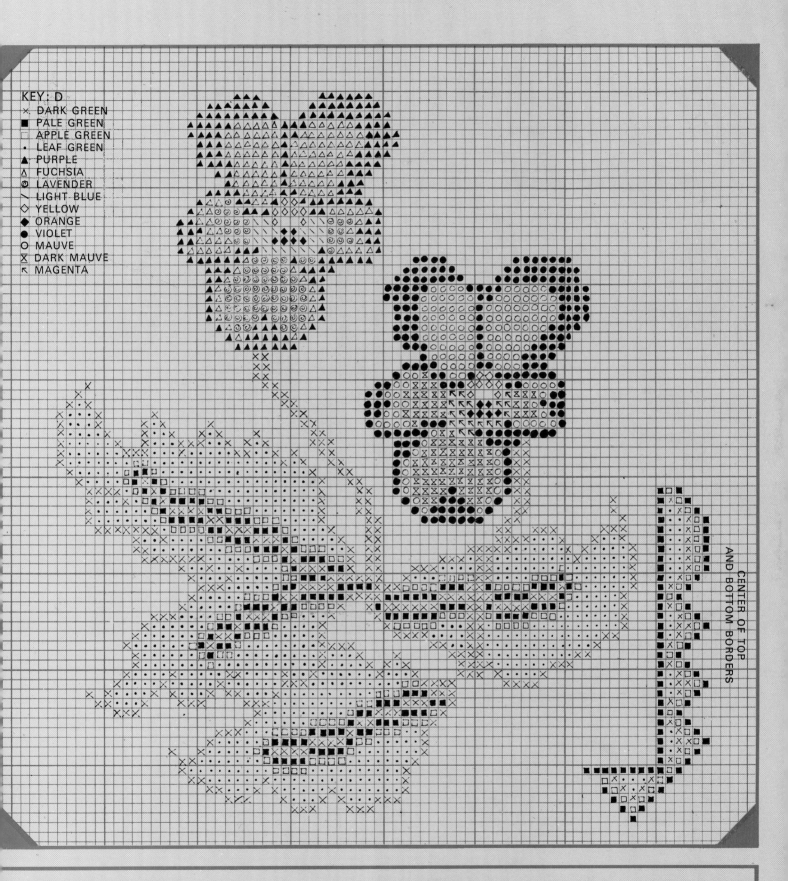

KEY: D
- ✗ DARK GREEN
- ■ PALE GREEN
- □ APPLE GREEN
- • LEAF GREEN
- ▲ PURPLE
- △ FUCHSIA
- ◉ LAVENDER
- ＼ LIGHT BLUE
- ◇ YELLOW
- ◆ ORANGE
- ● VIOLET
- ○ MAUVE
- ✕ DARK MAUVE
- ↖ MAGENTA

CENTER OF TOP AND BOTTOM BORDERS

How to work the sampler

Mark a center line on the fabric with basting stitches. This applies whether you are going to use a single motif or the complete composition. Always start at the center of the design and work outward because this makes the counting easier.

Each square of the chart represents 2 threads of fabric, so work the stitches accordingly, using 3 strands of floss throughout.

When completed, block the embroidery by dampening and pinning to shape. If you are going to use the embroidery for a tray, stretch it on firm cardboard cut to the right size. Fasten excess fabric on the back of the cardboard with masking tape. Cover with glass. If you are making a picture, take the embroidery to an expert for mounting and framing, unless you feel able to do it yourself. Instructions for mounting and framing follow in a later chapter.

Crisscross stitches

Cross-stitch comes in so many guises that part of the fun of working it is to find how many adaptations you can invent. When working a sampler, include as many different stitches as you can so that your work is interesting to look at. Or, use one variation of cross-stitch to bring a plain tent stitch picture to life. For example, an evening class student at the Royal College of Needlework in England was working in basic tent stitch on a mass-produced panel of a Spanish bull-fighter. She replaced the yellow tapestry yarn used on the suit of lights with gold thread, worked it in richly textured Italian cross-stitch and thus gave the picture her own individual touch. The illustrations on these pages have been enlarged beyond life size so that each stitch is clear—when seen in scale, the stitches will cover the canvas completely.

Oblong cross-stitch

Work in the same way as ordinary cross-stitch (see Needlepoint chapter 6, page 212) but bring the needle through 5th hole down from the top of the work. Insert the needle 4 holes up, 2 across. Bring the needle through 4 holes down.

▼ *Oblong cross-stitch covers the canvas quickly and has an elegant look*

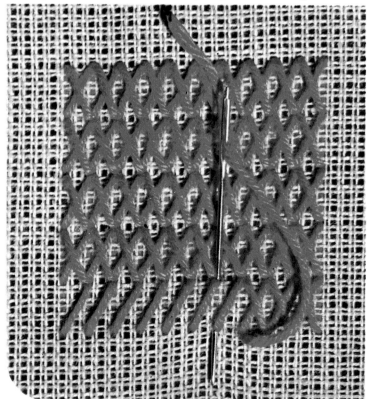

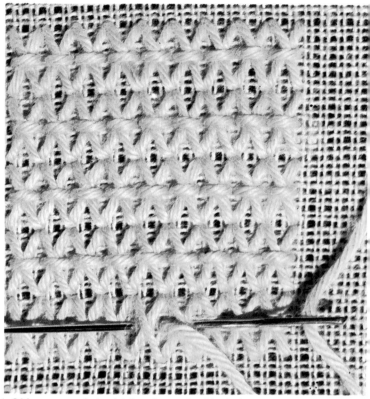

▲ *Oblong cross-stitch with bars has a chunkier look*

Oblong cross-stitch with bars

Begin by working oblong cross-stitch, then work bars making one row from right to left, the next row left to right and so on. Bring needle through 3rd hole down, 3rd in from edge. Insert needle 2 holes back. Bring needle through 4 holes ahead. Repeat to end of row.

Alternating cross-stitch

This filling stitch is composed of two cross-stitches of different sizes in interlocking rows.

Work from right to left. Bring needle through 3rd hole down from top of work. *Insert needle 1 hole up, 1 across. Bring needle through 2 holes down. Insert needle 3 holes up, 1 across. Bring needle through 2 holes down. Repeat from * to end of row. To complete the crosses work the return row from left to right. Next row—bring needle through 4 holes down and work each row so that it interlocks with the one above by working the top of each stitch into the same holes as the bottom of the stitch above.

▼ *Alternating cross-stitch, a filling with lots of texture interest*

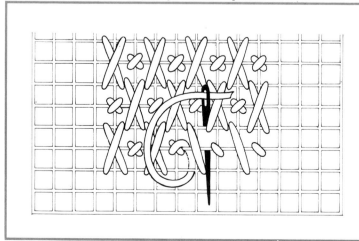

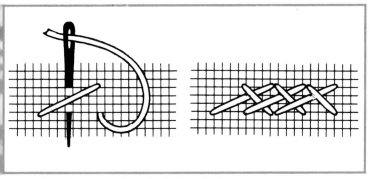

▲ *Long-legged cross-stitch, a simple but effective variation*

Long-legged cross-stitch

This differs from ordinary cross-stitch only in that one of the crossing stitches is worked over twice as many threads as the other. Bring needle through the 4th hole down from the top of work. *Insert needle 8 holes across, 4 holes up. Bring needle through 4 holes down. Insert needle 4 holes up, 4 back. Bring needle through 4 holes down. Repeat from * to end of row.

Double cross-stitch

In this stitch each star is completed before starting the next.
To work one star bring the needle through at top left-hand side of work. Insert needle 4 holes down, 4 across. Bring needle through 4 holes up. Insert needle 4 holes down, 4 back. Bring needle through 4 holes up, 2 across. Insert needle 4 holes down. Bring needle through 2 holes up, 2 back. Insert needle 4 holes across.

▼ *Double cross-stitch turns each stitch into an eight-pointed star*

▲ *Rice stitch can be worked in one color only or two contrasting shades*

Rice stitch

This is a filling stitch which can be worked in one or two colors (here it's shown worked in two). It consists of ordinary cross-stitch with the arms crossed by bars of half cross-stitch in the same or a different color.

Work the area in ordinary cross-stitch, then work the first row of bars from left to right. Bring needle through 3rd hole down from top of work. Insert needle 2 holes down, 2 across to the right. Bring needle through 2 holes up, 2 across. Insert needle 2 holes down, 2 across to the right. Repeat to the end of row. Then repeat the whole process from right to left to complete the row.

Italian cross-stitch

Work in rows from left to right, starting at the bottom left of the shape which is to be filled.
Work each stitch in 4 movements as shown in the diagram— bring needle through in the bottom left-hand corner of work. Insert needle 3 holes across. Bring needle through 1st hole again. Insert needle 3 holes up, 3 across and bring it through the 1st hole again. Insert needle 3 holes up. Bring needle through 3 holes down, 3 across. Insert needle 3 holes up, 3 back. Bring needle through 3 holes down, 3 across. Continue these movements to the end of the row, making a final upright stitch. Work another row above, also from left to right. This will complete the previous row.

▼ *Italian cross-stitch sets each cross in its own square frame*

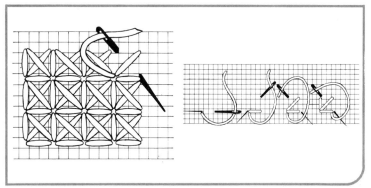

Lovely lace that's easy to make

It is a fascinating business to delve into the history of the styles, the materials and techniques which have always made needlework into an art. Tatting, for instance, is a type of lace made with a shuttle. Pretty, isn't it? It is not altogether certain where the name originated and there are several theories. It may have come from the French "tater," meaning to feel or handle. On the other hand, it may have some connection with the English word "tattered" or even "tattle," comparing the quickness of the shuttle movement to quickness of tongue! More than a suggestion of tittle-tattle occurs in the modern French for tatting, "frivolité."

Tatting is also known as shuttle-lace or shuttle-work. It is distantly related to the crafts of netting and macramé. It may also have been evolved by early seamen who would have been familiar with netting shuttles and would probably have used the knot for making rope eyelets.

Materials you will need

☐ Shuttles. These are now usually about $2\frac{1}{2}$in long and made of plastic, but were once larger and made of a variety of materials such as silver filigree, bone, mother-of-pearl, tortoise-shell or wood. The thread is tied to the center of the shuttle for winding.

☐ Threads. These should be firm and without stretch, smooth-running and fairly well twisted. Silk was used a good deal in the old days, but now cotton, such as fine mercerized crochet cotton or tatting cotton, is used.

☐ Hooks. A fine crochet hook is needed for making joins.

Formation of the half knot

Attach the thread to the center of the shuttle and wind it around until the shuttle is full, but without the thread projecting beyond the edge. This will insure easy running. Leave about 20in of thread hanging loose. The shuttle is always held in the right hand, which is only used to supply the thread—all the tatting knots are actually formed with the left hand.

Part of a handkerchief, beautifully trimmed and edged with tatting, shown together with shuttles, a fine crochet hook and a separate section of border

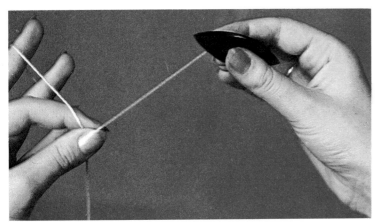

Hold the end of the thread between the thumb and index finger of the left hand and pass it over the other three fingers and back to form a large ring.

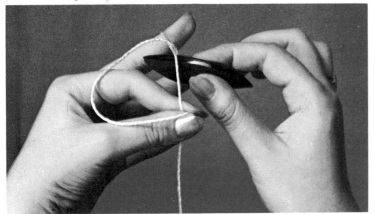

Then lay the thread from the shuttle in a loose loop over the top of the left hand and pass the shuttle from underneath upward through both ring and loop, from right to left.

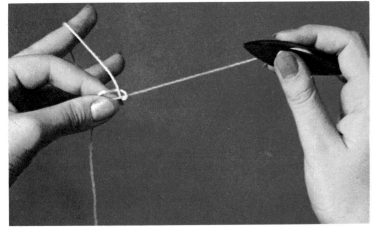

Now you have to do the basic tatting movement, which is sometimes the most difficult part for a beginner but is very easy and quite automatic once you have the knack.

Lower the middle finger of the left hand to loosen the ring, then stretch the shuttle thread horizontally to the right with the right hand and pull it with a jerk.

Then tighten up the knot with the left hand by raising the middle finger again, so that the knot slides on the shuttle thread.

This last movement is important and should be carried out perfectly without tightening the knot too much, so that this knot and all subsequent knots slide on the shuttle thread. As the knots are made, they should be held between the index finger and the thumb. Unwind the thread from the shuttle as you need it.

Bride's veil with Josephine knots

The Josephine knot

The half knot is the first stage of the basic tatting knot. The second stage, completing the basic tatting knot or double knot, is covered in the next chapter. However, you can use half knots on their own to make the Josephine knot, named after Napoleon's empress. To do this, make a series of four or five (or for a larger one, ten or twelve) half knots. Slip the work off your hand and tighten the shuttle thread to form a small ring. This particular knot is used as an ornament in the various laces.

Enlarged picture showing half knots used in completed Josephine knot

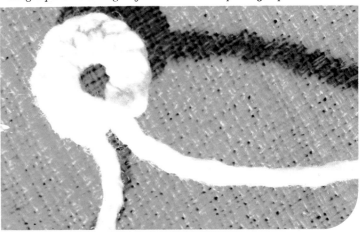

Focus on hems and belts

Making a hem is not just a method of tidying up to complete a garment. The length of a skirt is often such a fashion point that the eye is immediately drawn to the hem. Stitches which show on the right side, or an uneven length, are instant give-aways, so that a perfect hemline is essential if your garment is to have a professional look. Each type of hem has a definite function and gives the final hold to the outline. Some garments need extra weight at the hem to make the skirt hang properly, so the depth of the hem has to be considered. Garments made from extra-fine fabric, such as chiffon or voile, need a finely rolled hem for a soft, light, wispy look. Special hems like these come in later chapters.

The basic dress and skirt are finished with a conventional hem which is correct for the firm fabric used. However, it is the fabric, along with the cut of the garment, which dictates the method to be used for finishing the hem, and there are many different techniques for doing this.

Important rules for finishing hems

Here are some basic rules which must be followed whenever you are making a hem.

The most important point is to pin it up in the right way, for this is where you either make or mar your hem.

Always pin at right angles to the hem, however wide or narrow it is; never slant the pins or place them parallel to the edge of the hem. This could cause a shift in the layers of fabric you are pinning together and result in a twist in the finished hem which will spoil the hang of the garment as well as look ugly.

Always work with the hem lying flat on a table so that the weight of the garment is supported. By working in this way you will be able to see that the folded edge of the hem is straight. Or, if you are working with a curved hem, you will be able to see that the fullness is evenly distributed and directed straight toward the raw edge. If the fullness is twisted or forced to one side, it will make a kink in the folded edge and the hem will end up with a series of points in it.

Always baste the hem about $\frac{1}{2}$in from the lower edge. Make stitches between $\frac{1}{2}$in and 1in long, depending on the fabric and the length which holds it in position best. Never pull the stitches tight.

Always give the hem a light pressing (steam press only if the fabric requires it) and shrink in any fullness around the raw edge. Be careful not to press too hard over the basting stitches, as they might leave impressions in the cloth which are difficult to remove.

Always press with the hem lying flat on the ironing board, making sure that the garment is supported over the back of a chair so that it cannot drag away from the iron. Never pull the skirt over the ironing board, as it can pull out of shape when warm.

Always press the hem on the wrong side—it should never be necessary to press it on the right side.

▼ *The wrong way and the right way to pin up a hem. Always place pins at right angles to the hem, never horizontally as in the top picture*

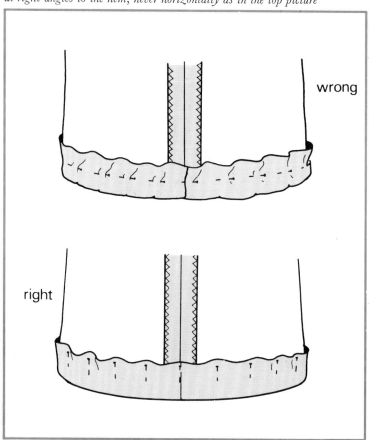

The flared hem

When you are faced with a hem which is curved and you have too much fullness to shrink, or you are using a fabric which will not shrink at all, make the hem as narrow as possible, sometimes as narrow as half the width of the normal hem allowance.

Then, using a small running stitch, gather in the fullness along the raw edge and draw it up to fit the skirt. Fasten off the stitches well so that the hem will not stretch again.

To finish off the raw edge on this type of hem, don't use the machine zigzag but overcast by hand. After a final pressing over the sewn edge, sew the hem in place using the invisible hemming method shown in Dressmaking chapter 7, page 136.

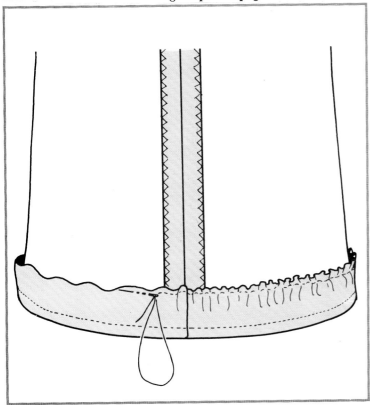

▲ *Gather the fullness on a flared hem with small running stitches*

The hem with a straight folded edge

When the hem is straight and you are using a lightweight fabric, simply turn under the raw edge $\frac{1}{2}$in and use a slip stitch to sew it to the skirt. This method applies mainly to fine cotton fabric or to special hems where extra weight is needed to help the shape of the skirt. It is a good precaution to press the folded edge first, though you must be very careful when doing this since it is possible to stretch a straight edge under heat and pressure.

The pleated skirt hem

When a hem has to endure a lot of hard pressing, as on pleated skirts, it is important to make the hem finish as flat as possible. You can never completely avoid leaving an impression with hard pressing, but by making the hem flat the marking will be less obvious. In this case, use a catch stitch. This means you do not need to overcast the raw edge except when the fabric frays a lot, and the hem will be as flat as you can make it.

The hem in thick fabrics

When you are working with a heavy tweed or other thick fabric, overcasting is not quite enough to finish off the raw edge of the hem — it should be bound. You can buy bias binding already cut and turned under which is ideal for this purpose, but make

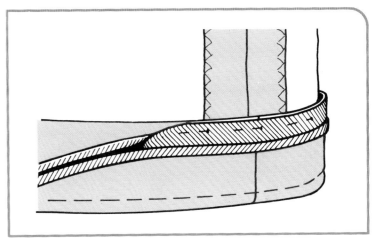

▲ *How to pin bias binding to the raw hem edge when using a thick fabric*

sure you buy rayon bias binding, as cotton bias binding is usually too stiff.

Prepare the hem in the usual way. Then take the bias binding, unfold one edge and pin and baste it to the outer edge of the hem, with the raw edges even. Stitch the binding to the hem, using a slightly longer machine stitch than you normally use for the seams. Fold the other edge of the bias binding over the hem edge and sew into position along the back of the hem with a running stitch. Press the bound edge before you begin sewing the hem to the skirt.

Although the stitches already covered are those most commonly used for hems, you often need a stronger stitch for heavy fabrics, because the friction between the two layers of fabric is greater. Therefore, to make the hem secure and also to allow for movement, use an invisible catch stitch and sew with a slightly stronger thread.

To do this, turn the hem edge back as for the hem on the flared skirt and work the catch stitch, catching the material from the garment and the hem each time.

In some fabrics you may find that the bound edge is too thick to turn back easily. Therefore, turn the whole of the hem under and catch stitch along the crease between the garment and the bound edge, as shown.

When you have finished and taken out all the basting threads, you will see how you can move the hem without it being loose or dropping out of line.

▼ *How to work catch stitch under a bound hem edge*

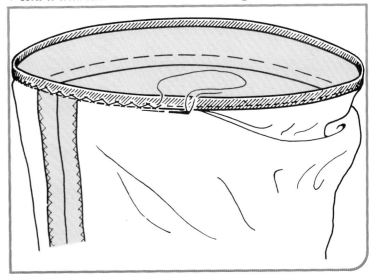

Soft belts, tied and buckled

With all the dressmaking you have done recently, you will probably have a little material left over, or you may even have a drawer full of remnants. So why not make a belt or two?

The simplest to make is a tie belt, which you can wear in a soft bow, loosely knotted or fastened like a tie.

Make a collection of soft belts—here are some ideas to inspire you

How to make a tie belt

First make a pattern for the belt using the skirt waistband pattern with the wrap extension in Dressmaking chapter 8, page 156 as your guide.

This will make a belt 1in wide, but if you want it wider just make a pattern twice the width you require.

Take the center of the waistband pattern, including the extension, as the center of the belt. You need to include the 2in wrap in the length, as the belt will be worn over other layers of fabric.

For the plain tie add 10 to 12in to each end of the pattern, but if you want to tie it in a bow add about 20in to each end, depending on the thickness of the fabric.

You can easily work out the length you need if you tie a tape measure around your waist and make a knot or bow. Mark the center of the waistband pattern by folding it in half. Then halve the length on the tape and measure this amount from the center of the pattern on each side.

Cut out the belt from single fabric along the straight of the grain, adding ¾in seam allowances all around.

Making a seam or joining the belt

If you have to cut the belt from two or more pieces of fabric, it is best to join it in line with the side seam(s) on the garment for which you are making the belt.

To find the position of the side seams on the belt pattern, mark off the length of the original waistband pattern centrally on the new pattern. Halve each section between the center mark and the end of the original pattern, then shift each mark 1in toward the center (the center back on the finished belt).

Cut out the belt pieces from single fabric along the straight of the grain, not forgetting to add ¾in seam allowances all around.

If you intend to tie the belt in a bow and want the ends to be even when tied, remember that one side of the bow takes up more fabric than the other. This amount is approximately 3in, depending on the thickness of the fabric. Therefore, if you are joining the fabric at the seams, shift the center back and side seam marks on the pattern about 3in toward one end.

How to complete the belt

First you must stitch the belt. Fold the material lengthwise, right sides facing. Pin, placing the pins at right angles to the fold to prevent the belt from twisting. Mark off the seam allowance with tailor's chalk and stitch the belt lengthwise, leaving the ends open and an opening about 3in long halfway along the stitching line, to turn the belt right side out.

Carefully press the seam open, because it must lie flat inside the belt and go to the center of the belt. If you leave the seam folded together in the crease of the belt, you will have a ridge on one edge with four layers of fabric inside it and a flat crease on the other edge with no seam at all. This will not only look ugly but will also make the belt roll.

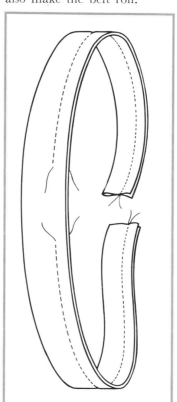

The tie belt stitched lengthwise

Be careful when pressing the seam open. Avoid pressing too hard and making sharp creases on the edges. You will only have to remove these creases when the belt is turned right side out, and this may be impossible with some fabrics.

After pressing, place the seam to the center of the belt and trim the seam allowance to ½in. Pin in place, then stitch across the ends, fastening off the threads carefully.

Now turn the belt right side out by pushing the ends through the opening over the

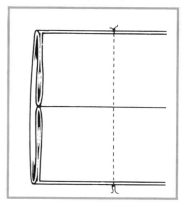

The stitched end of the tie belt

blunt end of a knitting needle or the unsharpened end of a pencil. Don't use anything with a sharp point—you will penetrate the fabric, push the weave apart and distort the ends of the belt, spoiling its shape.

When the belt is turned, fold in the edges of the opening along the seamline and slip stitch them together by hand. Pull out the corners gently with the point of a needle to make them square. Then edge baste the seams at both ends. Finally, press the belt from the back, making sure as much of the length as possible is lying on the ironing board. Again, do not use heavy pressure to get it flat or you'll leave a seam impression on the right side of the belt.

The buckled belt

For a soft belt with a buckle, again use the waistband pattern, including the wrap extension, as a guide for the belt pattern.

Mark the ends left and right; the left end is for the buckle and the right end slots through the buckle.

Remember, if you want the belt to be wider than the waistband pattern, just make the pattern twice the width you require.

Add 1½in to the left end and 4 or even 5in to the right end, depending on how much ease and movement you like. Before cutting the fabric, add $\frac{3}{4}$in seam allowances all around, except on the left end.

If you want the right end of belt pointed or slanted, prepare a cardboard template from the belt pattern to use after you have stitched the belt together lengthwise and pressed the seam open.

Place the seam in the center of the back of the belt and baste through all layers to hold the seam in place. Lay the template on the right end and carefully chalk around it. Remove the template, baste along the chalk line and stitch.

Trim off the seam allowance across the point to reduce the bulk and to allow the point to be clearly defined after

Buckled belt pattern and template

you have turned the belt right side out. Do not cut so close that the fabric will fray.

Turn the belt right side out, pull the point out with the sharp end of a needle, and edge baste the stitched end. If the belt is wide, you must also baste around the edges to make sure that the seam remains in the center of the back. Press the belt gently, remove the basting threads and press.

Buckles and how to attach them

In most cases, a belt is made to fit the buckle, but with a soft belt the reverse applies.

To prevent the belt from slipping back through the buckle, the buckle must fit tightly. So wait until you have made the belt before choosing the buckle, as you cannot judge before you have seen the number of layers that have to go through it.

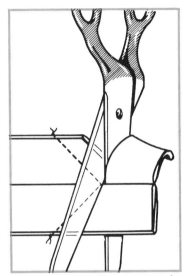

Trimming seam allowance at point

It is also possible for a soft belt to be gathered through the buckle, but you will have to be sure that the fabric is not so bunched that it will break the buckle bar.

To attach the buckle, fold the left end of the belt $1\frac{1}{2}$in over the bar of the buckle. Turn the raw edge under about $\frac{1}{2}$in and sew it to the back of the belt with firm hand stitches. Make a few stitches along the edges of the belt close to the buckle to prevent it from moving about in the turning.

To prevent the belt from loosening too much as you wear it, secure the end with a hook and bar to keep it in place.

Buckles with prongs

If the buckle has a prong, you will need to make eyelets.

These must be made by hand in a soft belt, because metal eyelets require stiffening as anchorage. Here is a simple way to make eyelets.

Use an eyelet punch, available from craft supply stores, to

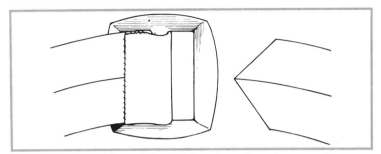

Buckle sewn in position and shaped belt end seen from the wrong side

make the hole. Select a hole setting slightly larger than the prong, because you will have to push the eyelet right down to the end of the prong to enable the buckle to sit well in the belt turning.

Make the eyelet $1\frac{1}{2}$in from the left end, in the center of the belt. When you have punched the hole, overcast the raw edge very closely, working over it twice to make sure you have caught all the layers of the belt in the stitches.

For the eyelets on the right end, select a hole setting the same size as the prong, or very slightly larger if the fabric is tightly woven.

Use a tape measure to find the position for the first eyelet. Again make it in the center of the belt and then make two or three more eyelets so that you can adjust the belt as you please.

Clasp buckle

A clasp buckle like the one pictured here can be most attractive and unusual.

To make the belt for the clasp buckle, cut out the fabric as for the buckle belt above, but this time add $1\frac{1}{2}$in to one end of the belt only.

Sew one end over the buckle bar as before and pin the opposite end in place. Try on the belt and adjust the pinned end before finally sewing in place.

Topstitching

You can give belts a more decorative appearance with topstitching. Either make one row of topstitches just around the edge or several rows down the length of the belt. If you topstitch the buckled belt, do so before attaching the buckle.

First, baste around the edges and then baste along the seamline through all layers of fabric so that you can keep the belt length under control.

If you decide to stitch several rows down the length, here is a tip to prevent the fabric from bubbling and the seams twisting. As soon as you see a bubble in the fabric in front of the presser foot, release the pressure on the fabric by lifting the presser foot, but leave the needle in the fabric. Replace the presser foot and continue stitching. If the seams twist despite this precaution, rip the seam and ease the pressure on the presser foot before starting again.

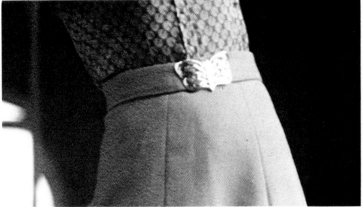

Turn a plain belt into something beautiful with a special clasp buckle

Junior fashion flair

Gaudy butterflies, pecking chickens and yellow ducklings. Children will love these bright, happy motifs appliquéd or embroidered on aprons, dresses or bibs. Use them individually, in rows or in groups. Make fluffy ducklings in terry cloth appliquéd to a bib; chickens on pockets with knobby French knots or bullion knots for seeds; butterflies in organdy, appliquéd and embroidered on a party dress; or just outline them in chain stitch or whipped backstitch straight onto the fabric in bright, clear colors.

Stranded floss or pearl cotton are the best threads for embroidering the motifs, and invisible sewing thread is good for slip stitching appliqué motifs neatly in place. Do be careful to choose color-fast fabrics for washable items (special care is needed with colors such as reds and dark blues).

Pattern Library

Basketful of posies

These lovely anemones look so realistic that they seem to spring out of the picture. This effect is achieved by subtle shading in tones of one color.

The design is worked in tent stitch on double-thread canvas with 10 mesh to the inch. When worked on this size canvas, the motif will measure about 10 inches square.

You can work it on a pillow cover with a navy blue background, frame it in an antique frame, or use it to re-cover a favorite stool or chair top. Use DMC Tapestry yarn in the following colors:

Basket
beige	7524
gold	7487
fawn	7511

Flowers
red	7107
black	
pink	7151/7153/7133
fuchsia	7155
purple	7257
mauve	7255/7253/7251
blue	7241
yellow	7435
cream	7431
green	7346/7344/7382

Background—white

Lacy look stitches

Knitting lace patterns will bring you compliments because they look so intricate. Actually, most of them are very straightforward. The designs often build up from an arrangement of openwork patterns made by increasing one stitch and decreasing another, either next to the increase or in another part of the design, so that the number of stitches is constant. If you are a beginner, you can use these patterns to make squares for ponchos, strips for scarves and oblongs for shawls which will not involve the shaping needed for a garment.

Shawls, ponchos, pillows and scarves are easy ways to use lacy stitches

Open-work ladder stitch

Open-work ladder stitch

Worked over a number of stitches divisible by 10, plus 6 (e.g. 46).
1st row (wrong side). P6, *K2 tog tbl, wind yarn twice around needle, K2 tog, P6, rep from * to end.
2nd row. K6, *P1, P into the first yarn over and K into the second yarn over, P1, K6, rep from * to end.
These 2 rows form the pattern and are repeated throughout.

Oblique open-work stitch

Worked over a number of stitches divisible by 9.
1st row. *K4, K up horizontal thread before next st to inc 1 st, K2 tog, lift inc st over sts knitted tog, K up horizontal thread before next st, K3, rep from * to end.
2nd row. P.
3rd row. *K3, K up horizontal thread before next st, K2 tog, lift inc st over sts knitted tog, K up horizontal thread before next st, K4, rep from * to end.
4th row. P.
These rows are repeated working one K st less at the beginning of each K row before knitting up first horizontal thread to move the crossed stitches to the right and so maintain the diagonal line. Extra stitches at the end of the row are worked into pattern when there are enough sts to form a new pattern.

Oblique open-work stitch

Ridged lace stitch

Worked over a number of stitches divisible by 6, plus 1.

1st row. *P1, P2 tog, yon, K1, yrn, P2 tog, rep from * to last st, P1.
2nd row. P.
3rd row. K.
4th row. P.

These 4 rows form the pattern and are repeated throughout.

Wavy stitch

Worked over an even number of stitches.

1st row. K1, *yrn, P2 tog, rep from * to last st, K1.
2nd row. P.

These 2 rows form the pattern and are repeated throughout.

Pimpernel stitch

Worked over an odd number of stitches, using two colors.

1st row. With white, K.
2nd row. With white, P.
3rd row. With yellow, K1, *K2 tog, rep from * to end.
4th row. With yellow, K1, *lift horizontal thread before next stitch and K into it, K1, rep from * to end.

These 4 rows form the pattern and are repeated throughout.

Old shale stitch

Worked over a number of stitches divisible by 11, plus 2.

1st row. K.
2nd row. P.
3rd row. K1, *(P2 tog) twice, (yon, K1) 3 times, yrn, (P2 tog) twice, rep from * to last st, K1.
4th row. P.

These 4 rows form the pattern and are repeated throughout.

Crisscross ladder stitch

Worked over a number of stitches divisible by 8, plus 4.

1st row (wrong side). *P6, yrn, sl 1 purlwise, P1, psso, rep from * to last 4sts, P4.
2nd row. *K6, ytf, sl 1 knitwise, K1, psso, rep from * to last 4sts, K4.

These 2 rows form the pattern and are repeated throughout.

> Forgotten the abbreviations? Refer to Knitting Know-how chapter 1, page 7, for how to work 'ytf', 'yon' and 'yrn'.

▲ *Ridged lace stitch*

▲ *Wavy stitch*

▲ *Pimpernel stitch*

▲ *Old shale stitch*　　　　　▼ *Crisscross ladder stitch*

Racy, lacy party looks

Machine knitting has come a long way in recent years for the good reason that it's quick and easy to do. This lovely dress shows a clever way to get a firm but lacy look with invisible thread.

Sizes

Directions are for 34 [36:38] in bust and 36 [38:40] in hips. Skirt length from waist, 41in.

Tension
16sts and 22 rows to 2in worked over stockinette st.

Materials

Using a Knitmaster 305 single bed machine:
23 [24:25] 75 yd spools Metallic thread, **S**
9 [10:11] 1 oz balls Spinnerin Frostlon Petite in mauve, **P**
9 [10:11] 1 oz balls Spinnerin Frostlon Petite in turquoise, **G**
4 spools Sew Gude transparent nylon thread, **N**
Two small buttons
One No.F (4.00 mm.) crochet hook
One spool of round shirring elastic

Note

The directions given are for one half only. Follow carefully, knitting the whole piece as one and shaping both sides exactly the same.
Where directions are given for binding off, the stitches at both ends can be bound off on the same row by using the carriage yarn on one side and a piece of separate yarn on the other side.

244

Any abbreviations are as normal and the number of rows for the larger sizes is shown in square brackets [ ].

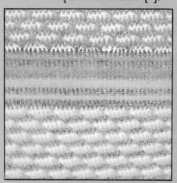

Pretty blend of yarns and colors

Work stitch patt from row 0 to 460 as follows:

Pattern	Rows
A	0– 62
B	63– 92
C	93–154
D	155–184
A	185–246
B	247–276
C	277–338
D	339–368
A	369–430
B	431–460

Back

1. Cast on 98[100:100] sts in **S** (i.e. 196[200:200] sts for full width, see Note).
2. K 12 rows. Tension 5. K 1 row. Tension 10. K 12 rows. Tension 5. Row counter to 0.
3. Stitch dial to 6. K 20[40:40] rows, dec one st.
4. K 10 rows, dec one st. Rep step **4** 43[41:41] times to row 460.
5. There are now 53[57:57] sts.

6. Work on right half only. Push up 17[19:19] needles to D position from center back, with carriage on right side.
7. K 1 row.
8. Push up 10 needles on next row. K 1 row.
9. Push up 4[4:4] needles on next row. K 1 row. Rep step **9** 3[3:2] times.
10. Push up 2[3:3] needles on next row. K 1 row.
11. Rep step **10** 3[2:2] times.

483 rows have been worked.
12. Push needles from D to C position, K 20 rows. Bind off.

Front

1. As for back to end of step **4**. There are now 53[57:57] sts at row 460.
2. K 7 rows, inc one st.
3. Rep step **2** twice.
4. There are now 56[60:60] sts at row 481.

Chart for pattern A

O					② ① W	S KII KI	P R	W ① ②		R
1	N	1	6	0	▼ 2 1		0	1 2	▼	2
2	P	2	"	"	" " "		"	" " "	"	"
3	S	3	"	"	" " "		"	" " "	"	"
4	N	4	"	"	" " "		"	" " "	"	"
5	P	5	"	"	" " "		"	" " "	"	"
6	S	6	"	"	" " "		"	" " "	"	"

Chart for pattern B

O					② ① W	S KII KI	P R	W ① ②		R
1	S	5	0	0	●		0		●	4
2	P	"	"	"	"		"		"	2
3	S	"	"	"	"		"		"	4
4	P	"	"	"	"		"		"	4
5	S	"	"	"	"		"		"	2
6	G	"	"	"	"		"		"	4
7	S	"	"	"	"		"		"	4
8	G	"	"	"	"		"		"	2
9	S	"	"	"	"		"		"	4

Chart for pattern C

O					② ① W	S KII KI	P R	W ① ②		R
1	N	1	6	0	▼ 2 1		0	1 2	▼	2
2	G	2	"	"	" " "		"	" " "	"	"
3	S	3	"	"	" " "		"	" " "	"	"
4	N	4	"	"	" " "		"	" " "	"	"
5	G	5	"	"	" " "		"	" " "	"	"
6	S	6	"	"	" " "		"	" " "	"	"

Chart for pattern D

O					② ① W	S KII KI	P R	W ① ②		R
1	S	5	0	0	●		0		●	4
2	G	"	"	"	"		"		"	4
3	S	"	"	"	"		"		"	4
4	G	"	"	"	"		"		"	4
5	S	"	"	"	"		"		"	4
6	P	"	"	"	"		"		"	4
7	S	"	"	"	"		"		"	4
8	P	"	"	"	"		"		"	4
9	S	"	"	"	"		"		"	4

5. K 8[11:14] rows, dec one st. Rep step **5** 5[3:2] times.

6. There are now 50[56:57] sts at row 529[525:523].

7. Shape dart. Push up 6[5:4] needles to D position on every other row 3[5:6] times.

8. Push needles from D to C on next 2 rows.

9. K 8[4:8] rows, dec one st. Rep step **9** 1[4:2] times more. There are now 48[51:54] sts at row 552[556:560].

10. K 4[3:3] rows, dec one st. Rep step **10** 13[15:15] times.

11. K 2[8:8] rows. There are now 34 [35:38] sts at row 610[612:616]. Work on right half only.

12. On selvage, continue to K 4[3:3] rows, dec one st. Rep step **12** 9[12:12] times.

13. At the same time (as step **12**), on neck edge bind off 5sts on next row.

14. Bind off 2sts on next row, dec one st on next 4 rows.

15. K 3 rows, dec one st. Rep step **15** 9 times. There are now 3sts. K 2 rows. Bind off.

Finishing

Halter neck

Join side seams. Put neck edge back on machine and cast on required number of sts each side, according to neck measurement.
K steps **3–7** of patt B (18 rows).
K 18 rows **S.** Bind off.
Fold halter in half to WS and sl st in position.
With RS of work facing, using No.F crochet hook and **S,** begin at top left-hand edge of halter and work 1 round of shell patt around halter and back edges, making 2 button loops on left side of halter, as follows:

1st round Work in sc. Join with ss.

2nd round *4dc into 1sc, 1ss into 1sc, rep from * to position for button loops, make 2 loops of 2ch each, continue in patt to end of round. Join with ss. Fasten off.
Sew on buttons. Turn first 12 rows to WS and sl st hem. With RS of work facing, sew a row of shirring elastic from top of front neck around back to other side of front neck.

Designing with motifs

You can make delicate lacy evening blouses, with or without sleeves, by joining together small crocheted motifs worked in fine cottons. The same pattern can be worked in wool for a warmer version, but since each motif will be larger, remember that fewer of them will be needed for the garment.

A blouse from crocheted motifs

The illustration shows a blouse worked in fine cotton using the wild rose motif, but if you prefer, you can use the forget-me-not or fourways motif instead. The wild rose motif, worked with a No.12 steel crochet hook and Clark's Big Ball Mercerized Crochet No.30, measures about $\frac{9}{10}$ in square after pressing under a damp cloth with a warm iron. You will find the pattern and full directions for the blouse on the next page.

The number of motifs needed for a blouse or other garment depends on the size of the motif, the bust measurement and the sleeve length. A sleeveless blouse would take very few, large-sized motifs, while a long-sleeved version would, of course, need many more. Once you have crocheted what you think will be the required number of motifs, lay them out on a large flat surface. Then place them together until you have the design shape you want. Remember that garments made with motifs have to be on geometric lines: The neckline will be square or 'V'-shaped, and the armholes of a

▲ *Fourways motif*
▼ *Wild rose motif, used to make the blouse on the opposite page*

sleeveless version will be straight, with perhaps one or two motifs under each arm to give width for movement. Don't be tempted to graduate the motifs unless you are really experienced—you'll find it much easier and more rewarding to keep the shape simple. Once you have assembled the motifs, check that the arrangement gives you the correct bust size, sleeve and underarm length you need for your size, and then pin the motifs together.

Now, using the same yarn and color as you did to make the motifs, stitch them together by using fine small stitches where the loops touch, taking only one strand from the motif to make the joins invisible. In some cases, motifs touch briefly and only a few oversewn stitches are required; in others, a small row of stitches may be needed. If you dislike the idea of being faced with sewing together all of the motifs at one time, it is possible to join them together as they are crocheted. To do this you must be certain, before you begin, exactly how you are going to arrange the motifs for the garment you are making. Crochet the first motif and work the 2nd motif as far as the beginning of the last round. Work

Forget-me-not motif

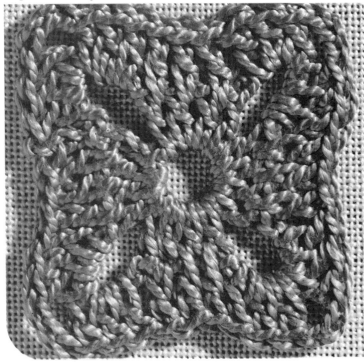

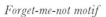

the last round, but when you reach a point where it needs to be attached to the first motif, you must work a slip stitch into the edge of the first motif. Continue the last round, repeating the slip stitch at all points where the motifs touch.

Fourways motif

Ch6. Join with a ss into first ch to form a circle.
1st round. Ch3, 2dc into circle, ch3, *3dc into circle, ch3, rep from * twice more. Join with a ss to 3rd of first 3ch.
2nd round. Ch3, 1dc into each of next 2dc, work 3dc, ch1, 3dc all into ch3 space, *1dc into each of next 3dc, work 3dc, ch1, 3dc all into next ch3 space, rep from * twice more. Join with a ss to 3rd of first 3ch.
3rd round. Ch3, 1dc into each of next 2dc, ch3, 1dc into each of next 3dc, ch3, skip 1ch, 1dc into each of next 3dc, ch3, *1dc into next 3dc, ch3, 1dc into each of next 3dc, ch3, skip 1ch, 1dc into each of next 3dc, ch3, rep from * twice more. Join with a ss to 3rd of first 3ch. Break yarn and finish off.

Forget-me-not motif

Ch8. Join with a ss into first ch to form a circle.
1st round. Ch3, 3dc into circle, ch7, *4dc into circle, ch7, rep from * twice more. Join with a ss to 3rd of first 3ch.
2nd round. Ch3, 1dc into each of next 3dc, work 3dc, ch3, 3dc all into ch7 space, *1dc into each of next 4dc, work 3dc, ch3, 3dc all into next ch7 space, rep from * twice more. Join with a ss to 3rd of first 3ch. Break yarn and finish off.

Wild rose motif

Ch10. Join with a ss into first ch to form a circle.
1st round. Ch1, work 31sc into circle. Join with a ss into first ch.
2nd round. Ch3, 1dc into each of next 3sc, ch6, 1dc into each of next 4sc, ch4, *1dc into each of next 4sc, ch6, 1dc into next 4sc, ch4, rep from * twice more. Join with a ss to 3rd of first 3ch.
Break yarn and finish off.
Sew two strands across center opening in either direction as shown in the illustration.

247

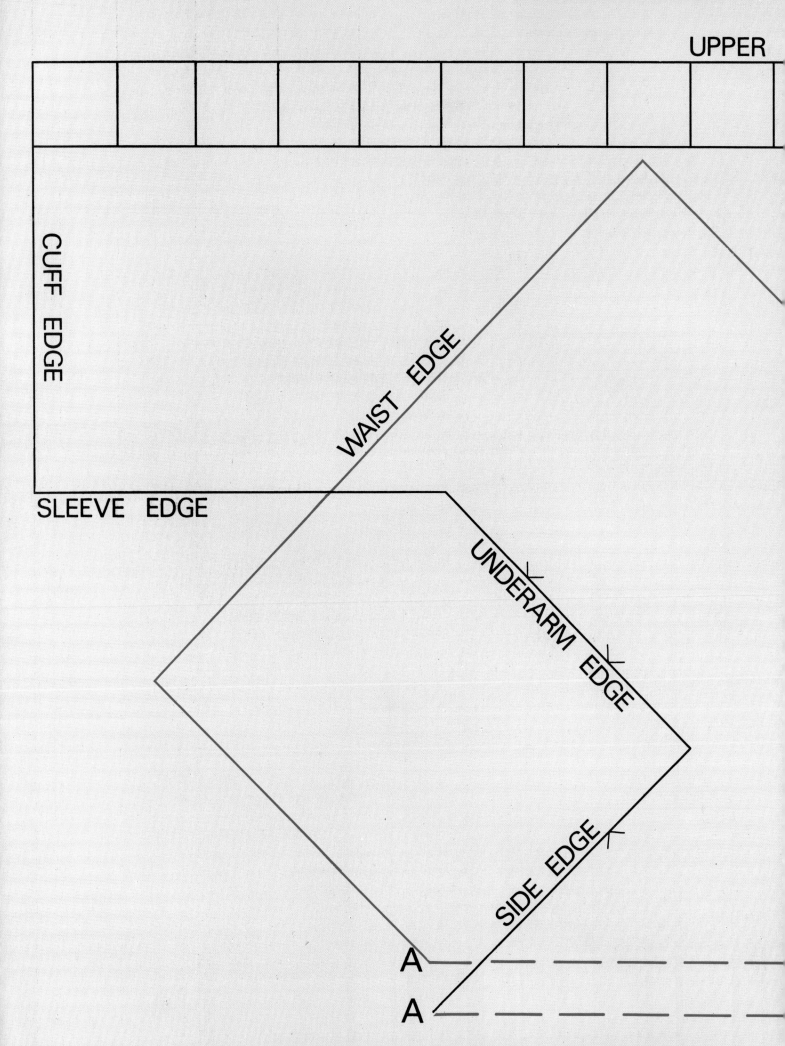

UPPER

CUFF EDGE

SLEEVE EDGE

WAIST EDGE

UNDERARM EDGE

SIDE EDGE

A

A

Crochet blouse

Don't feel that it is too complicated to form the wild rose motifs into a garment shape. Here is a shape and diagram to make it easy. Trace the black outline onto a large sheet of tracing paper, extending the cuff edge by two rows of motifs, or to the sleeve length required. Then place the tracing paper over the red outline, with the broken lines on top of each other and points A and A and B and B together. The shape you have traced is a quarter of the complete garment. Two of these shapes form the front and two form the back.

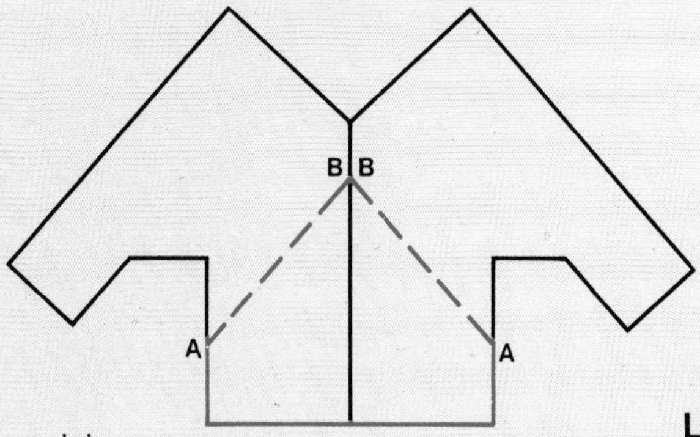

Beginning at cuff edge, join motifs for upper arm edge together to form first row, as marked on the pattern. Continue joining motifs to fit shape of pattern, leaving any half square spaces empty for the time being. Work four pieces in this way. Now join center fronts and backs together at the points where motifs touch. Join back and front together along both upper arm and sleeve edges. Join underarms and side seams together at points. The spaces between all points may now be filled with motifs to complete the finished garment.

This pattern can be used as a general guide for any size motif. If the motif you are using does not fit the exact shape of the paper pattern, be on the safe side by making the garment a little larger and then taking in extra width by seaming. If you want to use a motif which is much larger than those illustrated, place the motifs where you want them on the pattern, leaving any empty spaces along a seam edge. Join the motifs and then fill in any required width by working rows of single crochet or double crochet to form ornamental seams and to obtain the correct size.

CENTER FRONT

NECK EDGE

CENTER FRONT

The Feather stitch family

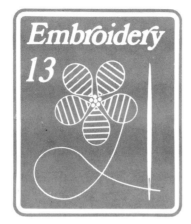

Feather stitch is attractive as well as useful and can be worked in straight or curved lines. It is one of the main stitches used in the decorative panels of the traditional smocks once worn by English country working folk.

The stitches shown here are all from the same family and are useful for either decoration or filling. Because of their realistically veined look, the lacy open feather stitches are ideal for filling leaf or fern shapes and they also look very pretty on hems and edges. When practicing feather stitches, lightly draw a central spine and parallel outer guide lines until you achieve the even stitching which is this stitch family's main beauty.

Feather stitch
Work from top to bottom. Bring the needle through at the top of the center line of the

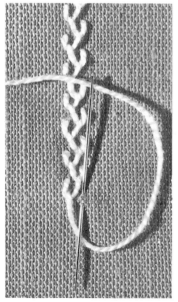

design. Take a small stitch to the right, catching the thread under the point of the needle. Continue making a series of stitches to the right and left of the center line, catching the thread under the needle each time. The result is parallel lines of stitches linked by a zigzag line.

Double feather stitch
Work in the same way as feather stitch, but take two stitches in each direction instead of one. This rather geometric stitch is very popular on the European continent.

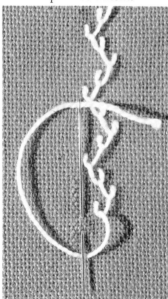

To achieve the more rounded, softer feather stitch favored by British embroiderers, angle each small stitch toward the center of the feather rather than working them absolutely parallel to each other.

Fly stitch
This stitch can be worked either horizontally or vertically,

but the basic movement for both is from left to right. Bring the needle through on the left and, holding the thread down with the left thumb, insert the needle at the same level, a little to the right. Bring the needle up below, but

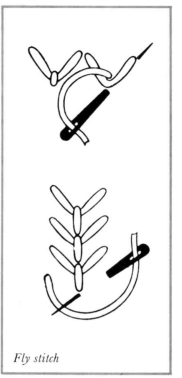

Fly stitch

exactly between, these two points, catching the thread under the needle. Take a tiny stitch just below this thread to hold it and bring the needle through in position for the next stitch. Continue in a horizontal or vertical line.

Cretan stitch
Work from top to bottom. Bring the needle through to the left of the center line of the design. Take a deep stitch to the right and bring the needle toward the center line, taking a small stitch and catching the

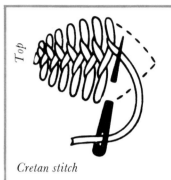

Cretan stitch

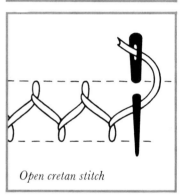

Open cretan stitch

thread under the needle. Make a second big stitch to the left of the center line and take a small stitch toward the center of the design, catching the thread under the needle. Continue, being very careful that each stitch is as even as possible.

▼ *Quill or long-armed feather stitch (top is to the right)*

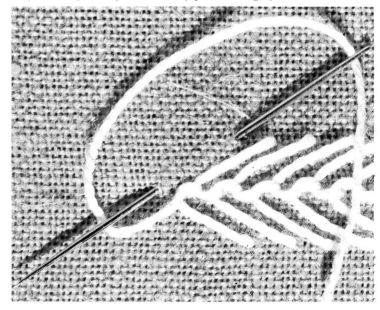

Cretan stitch makes a very effective filling stitch.

Open cretan stitch

Work this stitch in exactly the same way as cretan stitch, but from left to right, spacing the stitching at regular intervals. It is very important to keep the spacing even.

Quill or long-armed feather stitch

Work from the top downward. Bring the needle through on the center line of the design. Insert the needle to left and a little lower down, bringing the needle through again at the center, catching the working thread under the needle. Repeat, taking the stitch alternately on each side of the center line of the design, to form a quill.

Herringbone stitch

Work from left to right. Bring the needle through below the center line of the design. Insert the needle above this line to the right, taking a small stitch to the left. Then insert the needle below the line a little to the right, taking a small stitch toward the left, making sure that the needle comes up in line with the previous stitch. Herringbone stitch looks best worked very evenly so that the small stitches and the spaces between them are of equal size.

Threaded herringbone stitch

First work a foundation of simple herringbone stitch. Then, with a contrast thread (use the same color if you wish), pass the needle across the intersection of each stitch.

Laced herringbone stitch

This, again, is worked over a foundation of simple herringbone stitch. A surface thread is woven around the intersection of stitches to form the interlacing. The thread is woven twice around each intersection in the diagram, but it can be worked around as many times as you wish, depending on the effect you want to achieve.

▲ *This table runner shows one decorative way of using feather stitch*

▼ *Herringbone stitch*

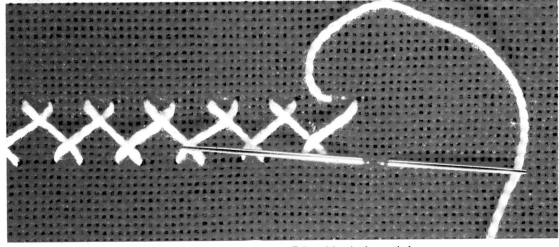

▼ *Threaded herringbone stitch*

▼ *Laced herringbone stitch*

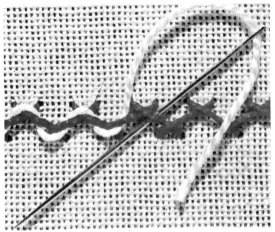

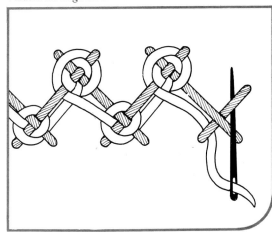

Satin smooth

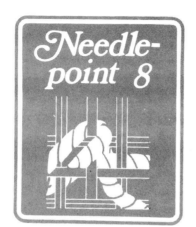

As its name suggests, satin stitch is smooth and flat. On a large piece of needlepoint, it is enhanced by the addition of rough-textured stitches around it such as long-legged cross-stitch. When combined with other stitches such as tent stitch or when worked to form brocade-like textures, different stitches are formed, for instance Byzantine, checker, cushion, Jacquard, Milanese and Moorish stitches.

Diagonal rows of satin stitch made interesting by using different colors

Satin stitch

This stitch is shown in several variations in this chapter, beginning with the simple but very effective square shape of cushion stitch. See how entirely different it looks worked into a zigzag, or into a square of four concentric triangles for a diamond. This last version makes a lovely stylized flower head.

The panel on this page shows you, on the left, how the stitch is constructed, and on the right, how it looks completed in a block of stitches. On the opposite page the stitches are worked with one thickness of thread and show a much flatter finish. They also show more ways of using different colored yarns to make striking and varied-looking geometric patterns.

Since satin stitch is quite long, crossing two, three or even more threads, it is not a good choice for pillows or chair covers because surfaces may catch and pull. When working with the family of satin stitches, make sure that the threads cover the canvas well, adding more strands of yarn if necessary. When using more than one strand, pull them all gently to insure an even finish.

Cushion stitch

Before you begin working the plump squares of this stitch, decide carefully which way the diagonal is going to lie. Its direction will make quite a difference to the overall effect. The clever use of colors will also alter the effect. You can see this from the color illustrations on the right which show a checkered pattern and a diamond pattern.

The diagram below shows a way of padding to fill the center gap. Work each square in the order shown, working the diagonal stitch AB before working sections 3 and 4.

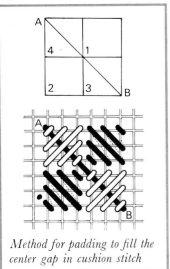

Method for padding to fill the center gap in cushion stitch

Half cushion stitch

This is cushion stitch worked over as many threads as required until it leaves the neat triangular shape of half a square. These can then be built up into diamonds as you see on the right of the panel.

Diagonal satin stitch

Diagonal satin stitch worked in bands over two threads (bottom left of panel). This stitch can be worked in alternate directions and over a different number of threads to give interesting zigzag effects. On the right of the panel diagonal satin stitch is worked over two and four threads.

Padded satin stitch

The area to be covered is first trammed and then stitched over to give a well-defined, padded effect.

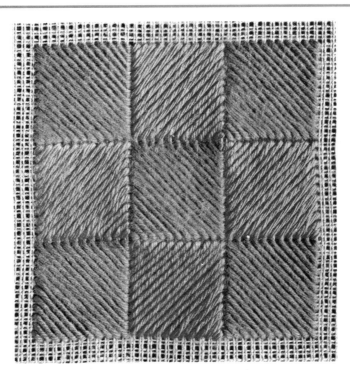

▲ *Square blocks of cushion stitch worked over eleven double threads*

▲ *Cushion stitch in diamonds*　　　▼ *Diagonal satin stitch*

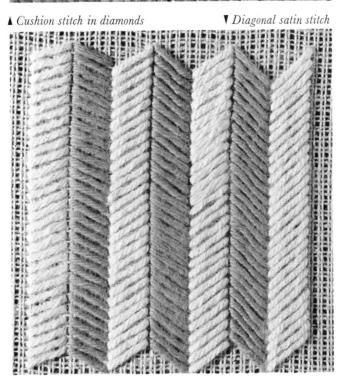

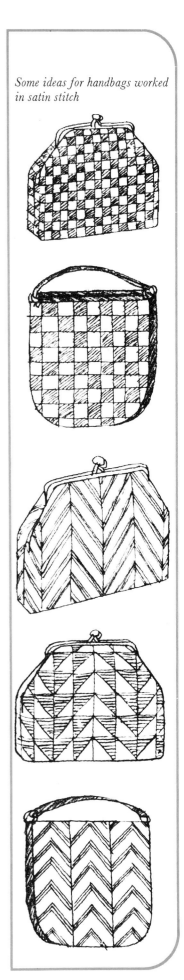

Some ideas for handbags worked in satin stitch

253

Double knots and picots

Double knots and picots are the natural follow-up to the half knot, and once you have learned to do these, tatting starts to become more adventuresome. You can work pretty borders using rings made with double knots and picots and oversew them to the edges of handkerchiefs, guest towels or collars. As a quick idea, join rings into a trimming and use it to encircle a napkin ring.

Reading a pattern

Tatting, like knitting or crochet, has its own terminology for which the following abbreviations are used:

ds = **double stitch**
p = **picot**
r = **ring**
ch = **chain**
sp = **space**

It is often necessary to repeat the same series of stitches or knots. When this happens, the beginning and end of the section to be repeated are each marked with an asterisk(*).

ds. In tatting patterns, half stitches are sometimes called half knots and double stitches double knots. Thus, ds in a pattern refers to either a double stitch or a double knot.
p. Picots are loops between knots.
r. A ring is formed by drawing up the basic loop of thread after a given number of knots have been worked.
ch. A chain is a length of tatting knots (not pulled up into a ring). It is often a way of going from one ring to another.
sp. A space is the thread upon which no knots are worked.

A picot joined to another ring and the second half of a double knot are the equivalent of a double knot. Patterns will omit instructions to make the second half knot, but will include this type of double knot in the instructions for the following doubles.

Remember, the thread must always run freely through the knots which are formed: If the knots do not run freely, they have been made wrong. Since you cannot pick the work apart easily, you will have to break the thread and rejoin it. Obviously, it spoils the whole effect if you have to cut and begin again.

Upon completion of a piece of tatting, the ends should be threaded into the lace. Upon completion of a motif, the ends can be tied and cut, although it is a neater finish to thread the ends into the lace and then cut them off.

The stitches

The double knot (ds)

The double knot or basic tatting knot is completed by the second half knot.

1. The second half knot is worked in the opposite direction from the first, covered in **Tatting chapter 1, page 234.**

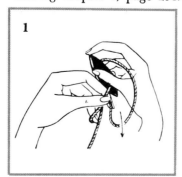

Wind the thread around the fingers of the left hand again, pass the shuttle (held in the right hand) from the top downward through the loop from left to right.

2. The right hand, as has already been explained, holds the thread and remains still while the left hand closes up the second half knot.

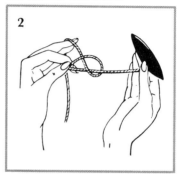

3. This second half knot completes the double knot, and the double knot is then repeated.

Double knot left loose

Double knot drawn up tight

Making rings (r)

Although tatting is easy once you have learned the basic knots, you must follow the work closely and be sure to keep careful count of the number of knots as you go along. When a given number of knots has been worked and you want to form a ring, release the basic loop of thread from the fingers of the left hand and gently pull the shuttle thread. This closes up the ring.

Making picots (p)

4. Picots are loops made by leaving part of the thread free between one knot and another.

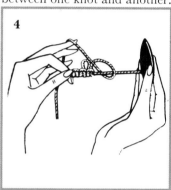

5. To make a picot, make one double knot, leave a space (usually about $\frac{1}{4}$in), and complete the next knot.

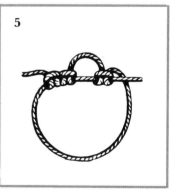

6. Next you simply push the two knots together to make the loop before you start the next knot.

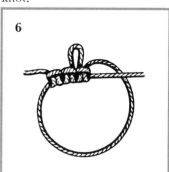

Joining rings by means of picots

7. Rings or pieces of tatting are joined together at a point where there is a picot. To do this, insert a small crochet hook through the picot of the previously made ring, draw

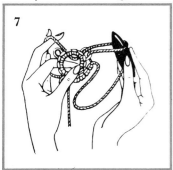

through a loop of thread and catch it with the fingers of the left hand. Thread the shuttle through this loop and draw up the thread before beginning the next knot.

8. This joining knot is used

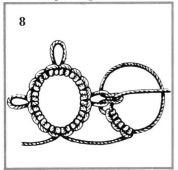

in place of the first half of the double knot and the second half is then completed in the usual way.

To make a simple ring trimming

This ring trimming is based on the step-by-step instructions in this chapter, and when completed it will resemble that which is shown above.

Make 4 double knots, 1 picot, 4 doubles, 1 picot, 4 doubles, 1 picot, 4 doubles. Allow the thread to feed in freely by stretching your fingers out and opening up the loop as required.

Slip the loop off the fingers and draw up gently to close the ring.

Leave a space about 1in long. To do this, wind the thread around your left hand and adjust the length of the space

as you make the next half knot. Anchor the thread in position with your left thumb.

Complete 4 double knots, join to last picot of previous ring, then work second half of a double knot, work 3 doubles, 1 picot, 4 doubles, 1 picot, 4 doubles. Close ring.

Make the trimming as long as you need it for your purpose and sew it onto the edge to be trimmed by the space threads between the rings.

Ring-and-Josephine trimming

This is a simple trimming which you can use as edgings for clothes, for lampshades or for special household linen such as mats, napkins and tray cloths. Here it is used in a slightly heavier thread to de-

corate a napkin ring.

Row of 5ds, 1p, 2ds, 1p, 2ds, 1p, 2ds, 1p, 2ds, 1p, 5ds. Close r.
*Reverse work by turning it upside down. Leave a short sp of thread (about $\frac{1}{4}$in) and work a Josephine knot (see Tatting chapter 1) consisting of the first half of a double knot worked 10 times. Close r. Reverse work again.

Leave another thread sp equal in length to the first and work r of 5ds, join to last p of previous r, then work 2ds, 1p, 2ds, 1p, 2ds, 1p, 2ds, 1p, 5ds. Close r*.

Repeat from * to * as many times as required to make the length of edging you want. Remember to reverse the work after each ring and after each Josephine knot, so that all the rings lie in one direction and all the Josephine knots lie in the opposite direction.

Pretty ring-and-Josephine knot trimming on a napkin ring ►

Dress-
making
13

Prepare
to pleat

Inside every small girl is a fashion expert in the making, and every mother ought to encourage her daughter to develop good dress sense. She may be tied to blue jeans and a T-shirt most of the time, which is all the more reason to encourage her to enjoy pretty clothes occasionally. The best way to learn is by sheer trial and error, which can be fun but expensive if you have to buy every item, especially considering how quickly children grow.

As no one wants a wardrobe full of expensive mistakes, dressmaking is the obvious answer. Here is a swinging pleated skirt any little girl will love to wear. Whether you add the shoulder straps or not will depend on the shape of her stomach. Later chapters include instructions for making more clothes for children, boys as well as girls.

A word about a little girls' fitting problems

Before you start making this skirt, it's a good idea to go over the basic shape of little girls and the skirt fitting problems that arise as a result of their shape at this age.

Generally, skirts will not stay up or they ride up and jut out so that the front looks shorter than the back. Pleated skirts look particularly clumsy because all the pleats tend to bunch together in front. Let's look at the reasons for the bad fitting.

If you observe the profile of a little girl's figure, you will notice that the curve of her spine through the waist toward the seat is concave and that her stomach is quite high and curves from the abdomen to the chest. This is typical of most very young figures. There is no waistline, and although there is a difference in the measurements around the body, the extra inches are taken up by the height of the seat and by the upper thighs.

The hip bones are not sufficiently developed to stop the waistband of a skirt from falling down, and the roundness of the stomach encourages the skirt to ride up if the waistband is tight. The only way to counteract this problem is to attach narrow straps to the waistband. These are worn over the shoulders and crossed at the back so that they don't slip down. For a child with narrow or sloping shoulders, it may be necessary to stitch a brace across the front of the straps to hold them in position.

Although the straps are strictly functional, they can become an attractive part of the skirt if made in the same fabric. They are versatile too, as sweaters and shirts can go under or over the straps. With the straps doing most of the work, the waistband can be made quite loose so that the skirt will hang better.

Although you might think an elasticized waistband is a good alternative to the straps, it pulls the waistband into the figure too tightly and only makes the problem worse. The reason for using an elastic waistband is to give easy expansion and not simply to hold up the skirt.

The pleated skirt made up in a woven synthetic fabric ▶

How to work out basic pleating

In basic pleating, the length of the pleat fold is the same as the pleat distance (or half the pleat depth). Therefore, you require three times as much fabric as the measurement you are fitting. This could be a waist or hip measurement, but in the case of a small child it is the waist measurement. Here's how to work it out.

How to work out pleating for the given width

In pleating a skirt from one width of fabric, the length of the fold is *not* equal to the pleat distance. Apply what you have learned about basic pleating, but remember, you are working on a given width of 54in. As you work it out this time, compare the two charts.

Use this column to work out the pleating yourself for a child's skirt in 54in width. Just fill in the spaces.

Basic pleating steps	Example	Given width steps	Example	Fill in
1. Take the waist/hip measurement loosely and add the correct ease.	For example: making a skirt for a 23in waist measurement with the pleats 1in apart: 23in + 2in = 25in	**1.** Take the child's waist measurement loosely and add 2in for ease.	For example: making a skirt for a 23in waist measurement with the pleats 1in apart: 23in + 2in = 25in	.....in + 2in = ...in
2. Multiply by three. This gives you *the amount of fabric needed for pleating.*	25 × 3 = 75in	**2.** You are working on a given width of 54in fabric. Deduct ½in seam allowance from each end.	54in — 1in = 53in	54in — 1in = 53in
3. Decide on the distance you want between the pleats and divide the waist/hip measurement plus ease by this figure. This gives you *the total number of pleats.*	25in ÷ 1in = 25 pleats	**3.** Decide on the distance you want between the pleats (for small children 1in is best) and divide the waist measurement plus ease by this figure.	25in ÷ 1in = 25 pleats	(Pleat distance = ...in) .....in ÷ .....in = ... pleats
4. Deduct the waist/hip measurement plus ease from the amount of fabric needed. This gives you *the amount of fabric to be divided into pleat depths.*	75in — 25in = 50in	**4.** Deduct the waist measurement plus ease from the amount of pleating fabric.	53in — 25in = 28in	53in — .....in = ...in
5. Divide by the number of pleats. This gives you *the depth for each pleat.*	50in ÷ 25 = 2in	**5.** Divide by the number of pleats.	28in ÷ 25 = 1⅛in	.....in ÷ ..... = ...in pleat depth

The all-around pleated skirt for 2- to 7-year-olds

This pleated skirt is made from just one width of 54in fabric and is therefore quite inexpensive to make. It's practical to make because it has a full round of pleats calculated in such a way that you can get it out of the shortest possible length of fabric. But before you can work out the pleating for it, it is necessary to know how to work out pleating in general.

Suitable fabrics

The fabric used for a pleated skirt should be crease-resistant, but able to take a sharp crease under pressure and steam.

Worsted wool, Dacron and a number of synthetic mixtures, linens and firmly-woven tweeds are good for pleating.

If you want a really hard-wearing, hard-washing and pleat-retaining fabric, you can't go wrong if you choose from the range of woven acrylic fibers (for example, Orlon and Acrilan). They can be machine-washed and still retain the sharp crease of the pleats, needing only the slightest touch with a warm iron to make the garment as good as new. What is more, you can pleat woven Orlon permanently yourself.

When you buy the fabric, always remember to ask if it pleats well and whether it needs washing or dry cleaning.

Fabric requirements

For 2- to 7-year-olds—54in width only, the skirt length plus 9in. Measure the strap length, and if this measurement is more than 27in, you will need an extra 3in of fabric.

If you wish to use a narrower fabric, you must allow the skirt length plus 3in for each extra width you cut to obtain the correct length for pleating.

You will also need two No.2 hooks and eyes, one snap fastener size 0 and thread to match the fabric.

257

Preparing the fabric before cutting

Before you start cutting the pleated skirt, it is essential that the fabric is perfectly square in the grain. To square the fabric to the grain, use the thread-drawing methods illustrated below, and cut the fabric along the line of the drawn thread.

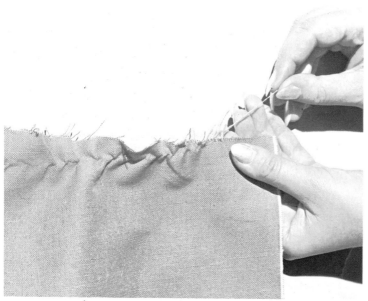

▲ *Finding the straight of the grain by drawing a thread out of the fabric*
▼ *Finding the straight of the grain by drawing threads from the raw edge*

If you are using a weave where the thread cannot be drawn, or it is hard to see the direction of the grain, the easiest way to square the fabric is with a tailor's square or set square and yardstick.

Carefully place the selvage along the straight edge of your cutting table and smooth out the rest of the fabric over the table. Be careful not to force it in any way. Lay the tailor's square along the selvage near the raw edge, then lay the yardstick along the top line of the square and draw a chalk line right across the fabric.

To check that the fabric is perfectly straight, repeat the operation about 10in farther down and measure the distance between the two chalk lines. The measurement should be the same on the selvage and right across the fabric. Cut the fabric on the line nearest the raw edge and brush off the other chalk line. The fabric should now be perfectly square for cutting.

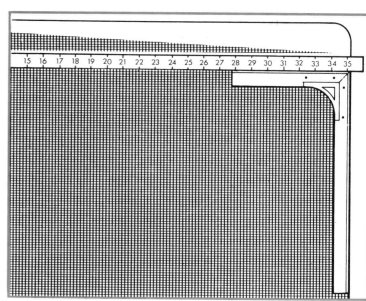

▲ *How to straighten the grain using a tailor's square and yardstick*

How to cut the skirt

Making a pleated skirt from one length of 54in width is so simple that you don't need a paper pattern.

Open out the fabric to the full width across the cutting table. Measure the length of the skirt along the selvage, allowing 2in for the hem and $\frac{3}{4}$in for the waist seam, then take this measurement right across the fabric, marking a straight line with pins or chalk. Cut along this line. Put the remaining fabric aside for the straps and waistband.

Finish the hem first, before you start pleating. Turn up 2in along the cut edge of the fabric and baste. A 2in hem is deep enough, since it is almost impossible to lengthen a pleated skirt after a lot of hard wear and washing, and moreover, you will be able to adjust the length sufficiently from the straps.

When you are sewing the hem, leave 3in at each end just basted—don't sew yet.

Press the hem and remove all basting stitches except those at the ends. Turn the fabric right side up and lay it flat on the cutting table with the hem toward you.

Starting the pleating

Have the pleating chart open in front of you with the measurements you need to use. Pleat from left to right, marking each pleat line with a line of pins.

Measure a $\frac{1}{2}$in seam allowance on the left selvage and make a line of pins.

As the skirt opening will be on the inside of a pleat, it is necessary to start with a half pleat, which means halving the pleat depth. Do this and pin off this amount from the seam allowance pin line. Now make the whole pleats, starting with the pleat distance followed by the pleat depth.

Repeat until you have marked off the required number of pleats, less one (24 in the example), all the way across the fabric. The last pleat (25th in the example) is the top of the opening, so for this you need only measure out the pleat distance. Turn under the remaining fabric and selvage.

Having measured out the pleats, check to make very sure that you have made the right calculations for fabric width and body measurements.

Fold along each pleat distance line, bring the fold over to the right to fall on the pleat depth line and baste down securely.

Make sure the hemline and waistline remain straight.

Baste the end pleat fold under.

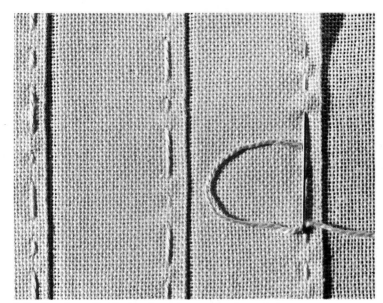

▲ *Basting down the pleats using a long and a short stitch*

N.B. When you're basting down lots of small pleats or any folded edge on springy fabric, use the basting stitches illustrated. Make a short stitch between each long stitch to give extra hold.

Pressing

Lay the pleated fabric, still flat and open, over a pressing board, making sure that the ends which extend beyond the board are supported. Press with a warm iron, using a damp cloth.
To secure the upper edge of the pleating, make a row of machine stitches just above the waist seam. Remove all basting stitches except those holding the end pleat, and press the pleats in again, more firmly, making sure you press each pleat in its original crease.

Stitching the side seam

To stitch the side seam of the skirt, lap the end pleat over the halved pleat depth you measured out from the left selvage and baste it in position.
Turn the skirt to the wrong side. Use the seam allowance pinned on the left selvage for the seamline guide, since you may have slightly more or less fabric in the pleat depth on the right selvage. Leave an opening 3in long at the top, unfold the hem and stitch the selvages all the way down.
Press the seam open for 4in, from the bottom edge, so that you can finish the hem.
Now snip the selvages toward the seam, just above the hem, and press both selvages together all the way up.
Overcast the snip with fine hand stitches to prevent fraying.

Finishing the opening

To finish the 3in opening, turn back the selvage seam allowance on the back of the skirt (the left end when you were pleating) to the length of the opening. Sew it down by hand using a catch stitch.
Snip the selvage on this side toward the seam so that it will lie flat. The front turning, or right end, remains just folded and does not need to be stitched back.

To prepare the waist seam

Make a mark opposite the left opening. Then make running stitches along the back waist seam, pull up the stitches and gather in one inch. This will give the skirt a little fullness around the seat to stop the pleats from spreading.
Gathering the fabric at the back of the skirt has caused the mark

opposite the opening to shift toward the back so, before attaching the waistband, you must make a new mark. Otherwise, the waistband will not go on evenly.
Measure out the distance halfway between each side of the opening and the mark opposite, and make two more marks.

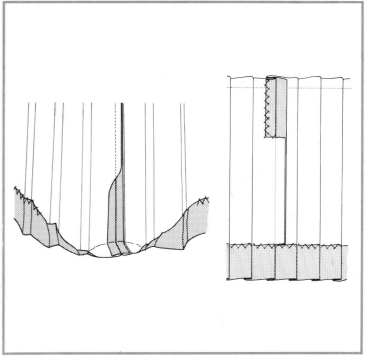

▲ *The side seam pressed open in the hem*   ▲ *Finished side seam and opening*

These are to indicate the center front and center back.
To obtain the correct length for the waistband, measure along the top edge of the skirt and cut a 3in wide strip of fabric the same length plus ½in seam allowance at each end. You will not need any extra wrap because it wraps in the depth of the pleat.

Fitting the skirt

Baste on the waistband and try the skirt on the child. Pin on two lengths of tape for the shoulder straps, crossing them at the back. Mark the lengths needed on the tape.
The skirt should hang almost free around the figure.
If you see that there is a pronounced drop at the back, try easing the skirt up into the waistband at the back. Be very careful, though, not to drag the fullness of the pleats from the sides of the skirt. If this happens, do not take the skirt up any farther.
Stitch on the waistband and finish with hooks and eyes for the fastening. Sew a snap fastener inside the fold of the opening so that it won't gape.

Attaching the straps

Measure the length of the straps from the tape used for the fitting and add 6in to the length. This makes room for adjustment for 2 to 3 years of growing.
Cut two 3in wide strips of fabric to this length. Fold them in half lengthwise and stitch them as for the soft belts (Dressmaking chapter 12, page 236), leaving one end open.
Turn in the raw end and hand sew firmly to the inside of the waistband about 2in on each side of the center front and center back marks on the skirt.
Now give the skirt a final pressing to seal in the pleats. Pay special attention to the pleat which goes through the hem in the side seam. The thickness of the seam inside the hem will need extra pressure to crease in the pleat.

Junior fashion flair
Country style embroidery

Embroidery gives a lively touch to even the plainest dress, so use these simple motifs to give a fresh look to your wardrobe.
1. Work the motifs boldly in chain stitch used either as an outline or, to give a bolder effect, as a solid filling. Padded satin stitch gives a rich finish, or whipped backstitch looks good and is quick to work.

2. Use motifs for appliqué work. Cut out the circles or leaves in a contrasting fabric, buttonhole stitch them in place and embroider details such as veins of leaves and flower petals. Six-strand or pearl cotton are suitable for finer embroidery, but for a chunky effect knitting or crewel yarn is ideal to work with.

3. Use the circular flower motifs for buttons. First trace the design onto material (fine wool, plain cotton or linen) and embroider with one or two strands of crewel yarn or pearl cotton. When the embroidery is completed, cut around the motifs, leaving sufficient turnings, and cover button molds in the usual way.

Jacquard stitch

This repeating zigzag design is worked entirely in satin stitch and shows an attractive use of color tones. Satin stitch in two widths has been used, which adds to the lovely effect of the design. This section has been en-larged so that you can see the stitches easily, but in fact it measures only 3 square inches.

Yarns shown here are:
D.M.C. Tapestry yarn colors 7541, 7540, 7772, 7771, 7745, 7742, 7484, 7436, and white. The canvas used is double-thread canvas, 10 holes to 1in, with tapestry needle No.19. The small satin stitch is worked diagonally over one pair of double threads and the large stitch over two pairs of double threads each way (vertically and horizontally) on the canvas.

Specially for 12-year-olds

If you have made a scarf or worked simple stitch samples, you will be ready to start on a mini-wardrobe for your favorite dolls. The brother and sister dolls shown here, Gregor and Sasha, are 16 inches tall. Perhaps you have some about the same size.

For their pants and shirts you need to know seed and stockinette stitches, increasing and decreasing, picking up stitches and how to make eyelet holes for the elastic and buttonholes. Easy directions for all these steps can be found in previous chapters. In later chapters there are clothes you can make for the dolls to wear over their pants and shirts.

You will need:

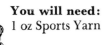 1 oz Sports Yarn

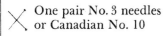 One pair No. 3 needles or Canadian No. 10

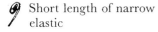 Short length of narrow elastic

Two small buttons for shirt straps

Gauge

7½sts to 1 inch over stockinette st worked on No.3 needles.

Note: If you are a beginner, keep in mind that it is most important to check your gauge before starting to knit.

262

Knitting Know-how 14

The given gauge of 7½ stitches to the inch can be achieved on No.3 needles using the yarn stated. If you can obtain this gauge in stockinette stitch, then it is safe to begin working the pattern. If your gauge is too tight on No.3 needles and you have too many stitches to the inch, change to No.4 needles. If it is too loose and you have too few stitches to the inch, change to No.2 needles. You must then remember to alter the needle size given in the directions to No.4 if your gauge is tight and No.2 if your gauge is loose. This point is vital.

Pants

With No.3 needles, cast on 37sts.

1st row K1, *P1, K1, rep from * to end.
2nd row P1, *K1, P1, rep from * to end.
3rd row K1, *ytf, K2 tog, rep from * to end.
4th row As 2nd.
Rep 1st and 2nd rows once more.
7th row K.
8th row K1, P to last st, K1.
For Sasha, rep 7th and 8th rows 5 times more. For Gregor, rep 7th and 8th rows twice more.

Shape legs

Bind off 6sts at beg of next 2 rows.
Next row K1, sl 1, K1, psso, K to last 3sts, K2 tog, K1.
Next row K1, P2 tog, P to last 3sts, P2 tog tbl, K1.
Rep last 2 rows until 5sts rem. Rep 7th and 8th rows 5 times on 5sts.
Next row K1, M1K, K to last st, M1K, K1.
Next row K1, M1P, P to last st, M1P, K1.
Rep last 2 rows until there are 25sts.
Cast on 6sts at beg of next 2 rows.
For Sasha, rep 7th and 8th rows 6 times.
For Gregor, rep 7th and 8th rows 3 times.
Rep 1st and 2nd rows once, then 1st row once.
Next row *P2 tog, yrn, rep from * to last st, P1.
Rep 1st and 2nd rows once. Bind off.

Legbands

RS facing, pick up and K 37 sts evenly around leg shaping.
1st row K1, *P1, K1, rep from * to end.
For Sasha, rep 1st row twice more. For Gregor, **Next row** P1, *K1, P1, rep from * to end. Bind off.

Shirt back

** Using No.3 needles, cast on 37sts.
1st row K1, *P1, K1, rep from * to end.
Rep 1st row 3 times more.
5th row K1, M1K, K to last st, M1K, K1. 39sts.
6th row K1, P to last st, K1.
7th row K.
8th row K1, P to last st, K1.
Rep 7th and 8th rows 5 times more.
Next row K1, *P1, K1, rep from * to end.
Next row P1, *K1, P1, rep from * to end.
Rep last 2 rows 3 times more.
Next row K1, K2 tog, K10, K2 tog, K9, K2 tog, K10, K2 tog, K1.
Next row K1, P to last st, K1. Rep 7th and 8th rows 3 times more.**
Rep 1st row 4 times. Bind off.

Shirt front

Work as given for back from ** to **.

Shape neck

1st row (K1, P1) twice, K to last 4sts, (P1, K1) twice.
2nd row K1, (P1, K1) twice, P11, K1, P1, K1, P11, K1, (P1, K1) twice.
3rd row (K1, P1) 3 times, K9, P1, (K1, P1) twice, K9, (P1, K1) 3 times.
4th row K1, (P1, K1) 3 times, P7, K1, (P1, K1) 3 times, P7, K1, (P1, K1) 3 times.
5th row Bind off 4sts, P1, K1, sl 1, K1, psso, K3, K2 tog, K1, P1, K1, bind off 1 st, P1, K1, sl 1, K1, psso, K3, K2 tog, K1, (P1, K1) 3 times.
Complete right front on these sts first.
6th row Bind off 4sts, P1, K1, P5, K1, P1, K1.
7th row K1, P1, K1, sl 1, K1, psso, K1, K2 tog, K1, P1, K1.
8th row K1, P1, K1, P3, K1, P1, K1.
9th row K1, P1, K1, sl 1, K2 tog, psso, K1, P1, K1.
10th row K1, (P1, K1) 3 times.
11th row K1, P1, sl 1, K2 tog, psso, P1, K1.
12th row K1, (P1, K1) twice.
Keeping seed st patt correct, work 34 rows on 5sts.
Next row K1, P1, yrn, P2 tog, K1.
Work 2 rows as 12th row. Bind off.
With RS of work facing, attach yarn to rem sts, K1, P1, K1, P5, K1, P1, K1.
Rep from 7th row of right front to end.

Finishing

Pin out the pieces evenly. Press lightly under a damp cloth using a warm iron.
Pants Fold in half and sew sides and legbands. Thread elastic through waist eyelets and sew ends to waist measure.
Shirt Join side seams. Sew buttons on back edging to correspond with buttonholes at ends of shoulder straps.

Meet Sasha and her brother Gregor. Their wardrobe is fun to make ►

A pretty useful pullover

A knitted pullover like this is a garment dear to the heart of the fashion-conscious American woman because of its great versatility. Wear it with a tailored blouse and pleated skirt, or team it with pants, a heavy sweater and a handsome belt. The interesting fabric stitch of this design gives a firm texture without being too bulky, and the deep armholes make it ideal for wearing over set-in or raglan sleeved sweaters. We made it in Unger Roly-Sport, which is warm but light and comes in beautiful colors.

Sizes
Directions are for 34in bust. The figures in brackets [] refer to the 36, 38 and 40in sizes respectively.
Length down center back, 26 [26½:27:27½]in.

Gauge
6sts and 8 rows to 1in over st st worked on No.6 needles.

Materials
Unger Roly-Sport, 1¾ oz. balls
5 [6:7:7] balls
One pair No. 6 needles or Canadian No. 7
One pair No. 4 needles or Canadian No. 9
Set of No. 4 double-pointed needles or Canadian No. 9

Back
Using No.6 needles, cast on 110 [118:126:134] sts.
1st row K2, *P2, K2, rep from * to end.
2nd row P2, *K2, P2, rep
264

from * to end.
3rd row As 1st.
4th row As 2nd.
5th row Place the right-hand needle behind the next st, K the following st, then K the first st and sl both sts off left-hand needle tog— called cross 2—*P2, cross 2, rep from * to end.
6th row As 1st.
7th row As 2nd.
8th row As 1st.
9th row As 2nd.
10th row As 1st.
11th row P2, *cross 2, P2, rep from * to end.
12th row As 2nd.
These 12 rows form patt and are rep throughout.
Keeping patt correct, dec one st at each end of next and every following 10th row 6 times in all, then inc one st at each end of every following 12th row 4 times.
Continue without shaping until work measures 16[16: 16½:16½]in from beg, ending with a WS row.

Shape armholes
Dec one st at each end of next and every following 4th row 17 [18:19:20] times in all.
Continue without shaping until armholes measure 10 [10½:10½:11]in from beg, ending with a WS row.

Shape neck and shoulders
Next row Bind off 5sts, patt 9 [11:13:15] sts, bind off 44 [46:48:50] sts, patt to end.
Complete left shoulder first.
Bind off 5sts at armhole edge every other row twice, then 4 [6:8:10] sts once.
With WS of work facing, attach

yarn to rem sts and work to correspond to first side.

Front
Work as given for back until front measures same to underarm.

Shape armholes
Next row Dec one st at each end of this row.
Work 3 rows without shaping.
Rep last 4 rows once more.

Shape neck
Next row Dec one st, patt 34 [36:38:40] sts, bind off 30 [32:34:36] sts, patt to last 2sts, dec one st.
Complete right shoulder first. Dec one st at neck edge on next 7 rows and *at the same time* dec one st at armhole edge on every 4th row 14 [15: 16:17] times more.
Continue without shaping until armhole measures same as back to shoulder, ending at armhole edge.

Shape shoulder
Bind off 5sts at armhole edge every other row twice, then 4 [6:8:10] sts once.
With WS of work facing, attach yarn to rem sts and work to correspond to first side.

Finishing
Press lightly.
Join shoulder seams.
Armbands Using No.4 needles and with RS of work facing, pick up and K118 [126:126:134] sts evenly around armhole.
Work in K2, P2 rib.
Work 1 row.
Work 5 more rows, dec one st at each end of every row.
Bind off in rib.
Join side seams.
Neckband Using No.4 double-pointed needles and with RS of work facing, pick up and K196 [204:208:216] sts evenly around neck.
Work in rounds of K2, P2 rib. Work 11 rounds.
Next round *K2, P2 tog, rep from * to end.
Bind off in rib.

Fancy trimmings

Crochet Know-how 14

Pompons and tufted fringe are trims which can add an interesting touch to wardrobe and household items alike. Give new life to pillows, scatter rugs or bedspreads by adding a cluster of jewel-bright pompons. Use a large pompon at the end of the cord on a window shade or drapes. A huge pompon will do, wonders for a plain wool cap—and you can add a matching one to your scarf! Tufted fringe, too, has a wide variety of uses. As you may have found, though, instructions all too often just say, "finish with a pompon" or "add fringe," but give you no details on how to go about it. This chapter tells you how to do both.

Small pompons

To make small pompons, wind lengths of yarn around two or more fingers. When you think you have wound enough for the size pompon you want, slip the strands off your fingers carefully and tie tightly around the center. With sharp scissors, snip both looped ends of yarn and arrange them to form a ball. It may be necessary to trim the ends so that the finished shape is neat and round.

Make cord belts with pompons or knot cord ends and spread out as tassels

Large pompons

For large pompons, you will need to use a cardboard frame. Decide on the diameter of the pompon you want and draw two circles of this diameter on the cardboard. From the center of each circle cut out a smaller circle: the larger this inner circle, the more wool you will need to complete the pompon and the heavier it will be when finished. If you don't have a compass, a cup or small bowl will be large enough to draw the outer circle and a coin or egg-cup is often a good size for the inner circle.

Place the two circles together and with one or more strands begin to wind the yarn around the frame as evenly as possible. When the center hole is almost filled, thread the yarn into a darning needle and continue until the hole is completely filled. To make a fat and well-shaped pompon, you must continue to work until the center circle is tightly filled.

When you have done this, take a pair of sharp scissors and begin to cut the strands of yarn at the outside edge, working in line with the edge of the cardboard and placing the scissors between the cardboard circles. Once you have cut all the strands, you are ready to begin the final stage.

Gently, with the tips of the scissors, begin to open the cardboard rings until they are far enough apart for you to tie a strong strand of yarn tightly around all the threads where they pass through the center of the rings. If you plan to sew the pompon onto a garment, you may like to leave the ends of the tying yarn hanging so that you can use them for sewing on. Once the center is tied, continue to remove both rings of cardboard.

When you have finished this step, fluff the pompon into a complete ball and trim the uneven ends.

For a multi-colored pompon, work all the colors together. If you want a striped effect, work around the ring in one color and then in another. Or, work in sections of one color at a time if you want to make a patchwork pompon.

Tufted fringing

From the illustration, you can see how to give a simple shawl a soft, frothy edge by adding a tufted fringe.

The number and size of the tufts on each strand, as well as the distance between the tufts, can be altered according to your own taste. You can make a short, thick fringe by working only a few chain stitches between each tuft, or a deeper, more delicate fringe by spacing the tufts much farther apart—all you need to do is simply work more chain stitches between the tufts.

Begin by preparing the tufts. Decide on the size you want and cut a piece of cardboard this width and several inches long. Then wind the yarn around the full length of the cardboard and cut along the edges. If each tuft on the strand is to be a different width, then you will need one piece of cardboard for each width. The illustrations on the opposite page show a strand of red wool made with three different sized tufts.

Now prepare the strands. Begin the first strand by making 9 chain stitches with a crochet hook. Open out the last chain stitch and place the desired number of threads in the loop. When the tuft is in place, pull the open stitch tight to grip all the threads in the center of the tuft. Continue by making 9 chain stitches before inserting the next tuft.

Complete the number of tufts you want in this way and join the strand, when completed, to the edge of the work with a slip stitch. Cut the yarn and fasten off the ends. Join other strands at even intervals along the edge to be trimmed. Finally, when the fringe is completed, you can anchor each tuft even more securely by working several small stitches through the center of tuft and chain with a fine, matching sewing thread or yarn.

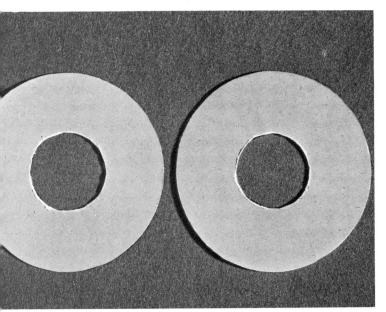

▲ *Frame for making big pompons: two cut-out circles of cardboard*

▲ *Winding the yarn onto the frame*   ▼ *The finished pompon*

▲ *Working the chain between tufts*   ▲ *Joining a tuft to the chain*

▼ *A shawl made glamorous by the addition of tufted fringe*

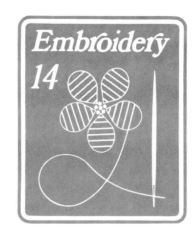

Tambour work on caftans

Tambour work first originated many centuries ago in the Orient. It reached Europe in the mid 18th century and was introduced to Britain during the early 19th century. As both hands have to be free to do the work, the embroidery was worked in a circular tambour frame (hence the name) and was done on net or fine muslin. Similar to chain stitch in appearance, tambour stitch is formed by the use of a tambour hook or a fine crochet hook.

This versatile stitch can be used in various ways to create greatly contrasting effects. It can be used purely as an embroidery stitch as seen on traditional Indian embroidery, when it is worked in rich colors on fine silk or cotton fabric and frequently enriched with the addition of paillettes or mirrors. A variety of yarns can be used such as very fine wools, cottons, and silk—yarns which come on a spool are preferable, as a free running thread is needed and too many joinings should be avoided. Tambour stitch can also be used as a couching stitch with a fine thread such as machine embroidery cotton worked in a zigzag motion to secure heavier yarns in place. Finally, it is an ideal method for attaching beads and sequins.

The embroidery for the caftan on this page has been specially designed for Creative Hands and the pattern for tracing appears on the next two pages. It is worked completely in simple chain stitch, but you could use a chain stitch variation or any line stitch, plain or whipped. For really quick results, tambour stitch is particularly suitable for dress embroidery. If neither of these suggestions appeals to your taste, later chapters of Creative Hands contain a special section on the techniques of machine embroidery.

Method of working tambour stitch

It is essential to work this type of embroidery in a frame with a stand since both hands need to be free, one to hold the hook and the other to hold the thread. The thread must be placed in a position where it can run freely off the spool. If you are using a frame which is assembled with cotter pins, replace one of the pins with a long nail, over which the spool of yarn can be placed. The hook is used in the same way as a crochet hook, but the chain stitches are made through the fabric. Holding the hook in the right hand and the thread in the left hand, insert the hook into the fabric on the line of design. Pick up a loop through the fabric. Insert the hook a little distance ahead, depending on how long you want to make the stitches, and draw through another loop. Continue in this way until the work is finished. It is advisable to secure the starting and ending points of the work very firmly; otherwise, the ends could work loose and cause the entire embroidery to come undone.

Broad or reversed chain

Make a small running stitch, then bring the needle out to the required depth of the stitch. Slide the needle back under the running stitch, inserting it once again where it last came through the fabric. Make another stitch, slide the needle under the two threads of the previous stitch and continue. This stitch is most effective worked in a thick thread with a small stitch.

Dress embroidery

Always plan dress embroidery to follow a neck line, a sleeve shape or a hem, as shown here, so that the design appears as an integral part of the garment.

◄ *The pattern for embroidering this smart caftan is on the next two pages*

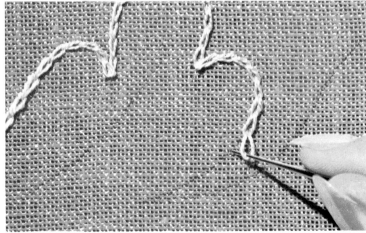

Tambour stitch: ▲ *Insert hook in fabric* ▼ *Pull up loop through fabric*

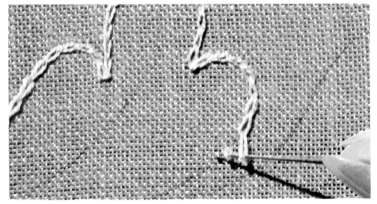

▼ *Draw loop through previous loop and you are ready to insert hook again*

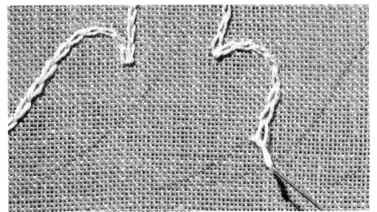

▼ *Broad or reversed chain stitch: See chapter 9, pg. 168 for other chain stitches.*

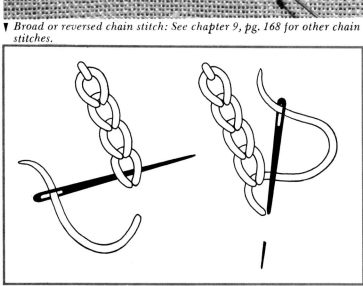

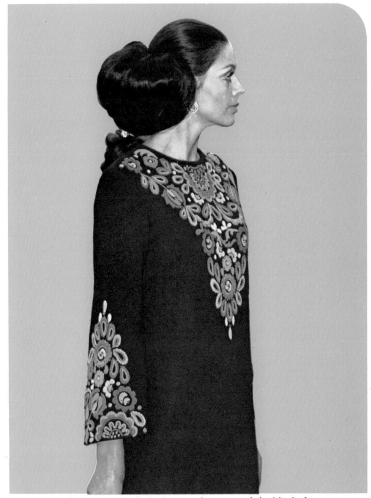

Rich embroidery looks particularly stunning on a plain black dress

center line

center line

1

2

3

center line

cen...

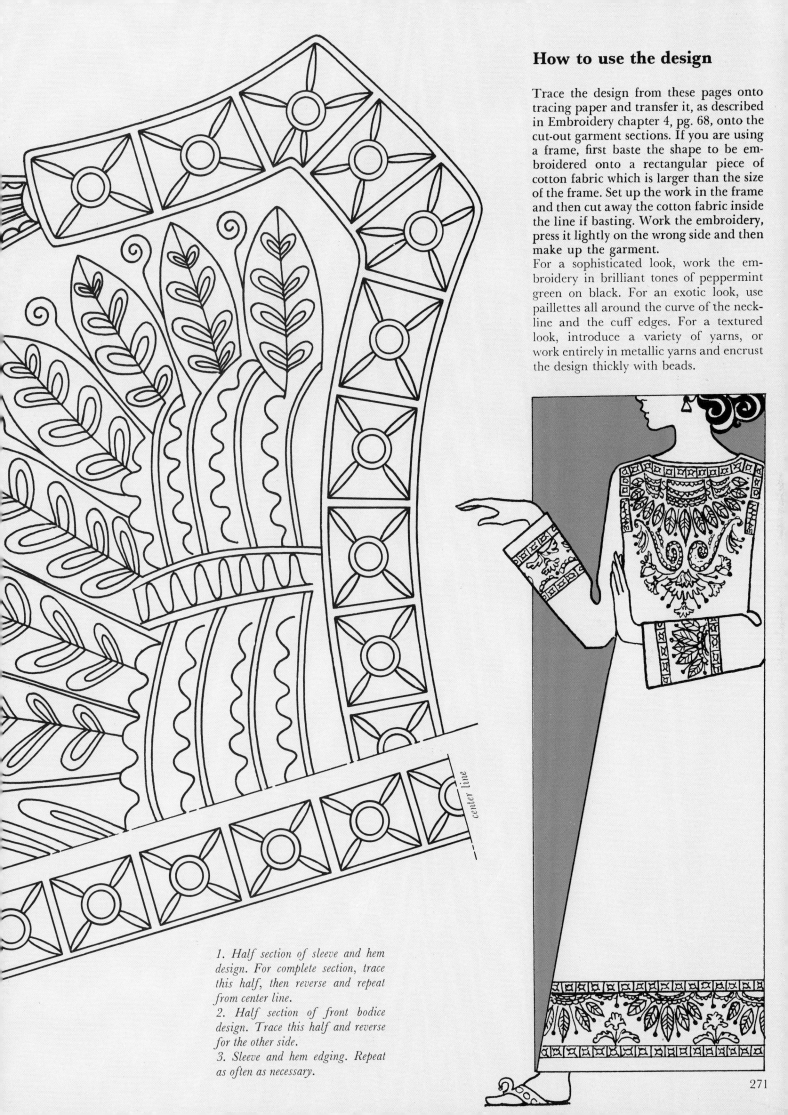

How to use the design

Trace the design from these pages onto tracing paper and transfer it, as described in Embroidery chapter 4, pg. 68, onto the cut-out garment sections. If you are using a frame, first baste the shape to be embroidered onto a rectangular piece of cotton fabric which is larger than the size of the frame. Set up the work in the frame and then cut away the cotton fabric inside the line if basting. Work the embroidery, press it lightly on the wrong side and then make up the garment.

For a sophisticated look, work the embroidery in brilliant tones of peppermint green on black. For an exotic look, use paillettes all around the curve of the neck-line and the cuff edges. For a textured look, introduce a variety of yarns, or work entirely in metallic yarns and encrust the design thickly with beads.

center line

1. Half section of sleeve and hem design. For complete section, trace this half, then reverse and repeat from center line.
2. Half section of front bodice design. Trace this half and reverse for the other side.
3. Sleeve and hem edging. Repeat as often as necessary.

For the apple of your eye

A pincushion is a good way to begin working from a charted design. Using a chart is less expensive than buying a painted or trammed canvas, which will confine you to the most commercially available designs, while a charted picture gives you the opportunity of picking your own colors and building up your own designs. For instance, you can repeat the apple motif given opposite at random all over a cushion, or turn it into a yellow Golden Delicious or a green Granny Smith.

Using a chart

A chart demands a little concentration when it comes to plotting the outlines, but once these are worked out the rest is easy. Start by finding the center of the chart. In this case you need to find the center of the apple motif, so count the number of squares from top to bottom and from side to side, divide each total by half and mark the center. Then fold the canvas in half both ways and mark its center with a pencil or lines of basting. Start counting and stitching from the center. Each square on the chart corresponds to one thread intersection on the canvas.
If there are large areas of color to be filled in, mark the outline and the smaller areas first, and then fill in the larger areas.

Two pincushions to work: one from the chart opposite, one row by row

The right stitch for the right texture

Any design loses impact if all areas are worked in the same texture, that is, all rough or all smooth. For the most pleasing effect, it is important to separate areas of the design into smooth, medium and rough textures. (Tent, gobelin, straight and satin stitches are all smooth. Cross-, rice and star stitches are semi-rough. Double cross-, oblong and tufted stitches are very rough.) Some stitches lend themselves to particular textures and shapes. For instance, diagonal bricking and Smyrna cross-stitch have a good texture for walls and brickwork, herringbone fillings interpret water very well and Surrey stitch is good for the curves of flowers or for furry textures. Tent and Gobelin stitches clarify the line of a design and for any form of intricate, realistic shading, nothing beats tent stitch.
Strong texture often looks most effective when it is used sparingly. For example, you could work just the mane and tail of a horse in a rough textured stitch, or use different stitches for flower centers and leaves, or the underside of a fish.

Apple pincushion

This plump apple pincushion uses lustrous cushion stitch to interpret the shiny apple, rough reinforced cross-stitch for the gnarled leaf, and precise tent stitch for the neat shape of the stem and eye.

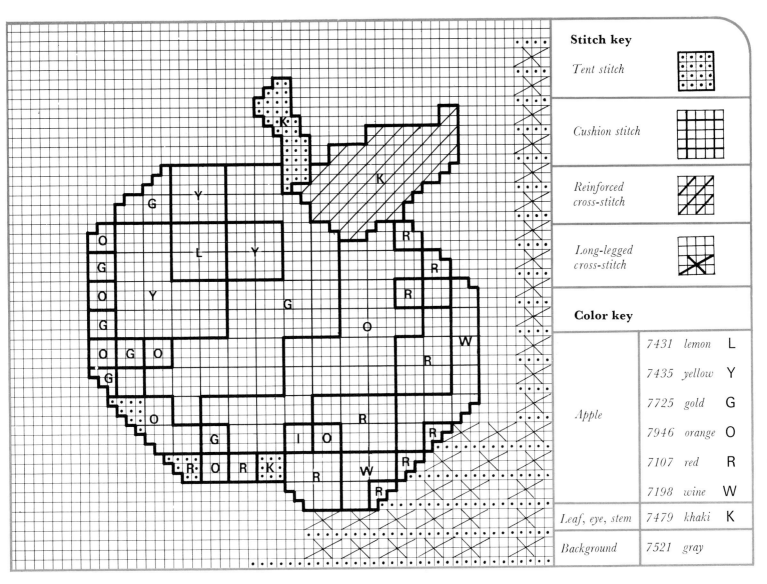

Stitch key

Tent stitch	
Cushion stitch	
Reinforced cross-stitch	
Long-legged cross-stitch	

Color key

Apple	7431	*lemon*	L
	7435	*yellow*	Y
	7725	*gold*	G
	7946	*orange*	O
	7107	*red*	R
	7198	*wine*	W
Leaf, eye, stem	7479	*khaki*	K
Background	7521	*gray*	

You will need

- ☐ Single-weave canvas 10in by 10in, 14 threads to the in. (Finished size about 4in square.)
- ☐ No.20 tapestry needle and a sharp needle for finishing.
- ☐ Velvet or other backing material, 6in by 6in.
- ☐ One skein each of D.M.C. Tapestry yarns 7431, 7435, 7725, 7946, 7107, 7198, 7479; and two skeins of 7521.
- ☐ 18in of cord for trimming.
- ☐ Sawdust from the lumberyard for filling.

To work the apple

Prevent the canvas from fraying by binding the edges with masking tape. On the chart, each square represents 1 canvas thread crossing which is to be covered by a single tent stitch.

Apple: Work in cushion stitch in groups of four over 3 threads.

Eye and stem: Work in tent stitch over 1 thread.

Leaf: Work in reinforced cross-stitch (i.e. cross-stitch worked twice over) over 2 threads. This insures that there is a good coverage of the canvas.

Background: Work in alternate rows of long-legged cross-stitch worked over 2 threads, and tent stitch worked over 1 thread.

N.B. To clarify chart, background symbols do not cover entire area.

Stretching the canvas back into shape

When the design is completed, stretch the canvas (see Needlepoint chapter 5, page 112) and trim off excess canvas, leaving ⅝in seam allowances.

Finishing

To back the cushion, cut a square of velvet to the size of the trimmed canvas. Baste the seam allowances on the wrong side to make a neat, accurate square. Pin velvet to canvas, wrong sides together, and whip the velvet firmly into place, sewing into the outer row of needlepoint stitches.

Leave center of one side open for stuffing.

Sawdust is the stuffing which best allows pins to be pushed in easily. Pack it in very tightly—a teaspoon will help. Close the opening with pins and whip tightly when fully stuffed. Brush off any sawdust left lying on the pincushion. Sew cord all around the edge, covering the seam.

Square pincushion

The square pincushion is worked in delightful, bright, rich colors in a simple geometric design using a variety of lovely stitches. Work it outward from a center block of 4 cushion stitches in rows as follows: 2 rows tent stitch, 1 row cross-stitch, 1 row Smyrna cross-stitch, 1 row satin stitch, 1 row oblong cross-stitch with bars, 1 row long-legged cross-stitch, 1 row Smyrna cross-stitch, 1 row satin stitch, 1 row cross-stitch. For the sides, work 1 row oblong cross-stitch with bars, 1 row long-legged cross-stitch, 1 row Smyrna cross-stitch, 1 row long-legged cross-stitch, 1 row oblong cross-stitch with bars. Work long-legged cross-stitching for seams.

Toy making 2

It's lambing time

This merry lamb makes a charming toy or ornament for a baby's room. The instructions suggest colored felts, but synthetic fur fabric or printed cotton are also suitable. If the lamb is for a baby, it must be washable, so choose a material which is colorfast, washable, shrink-proof and very hardy!

You will need
To make a white felt lamb 9½in high
☐ Two 12in squares white felt
☐ Scraps of colored felt in pink, red, yellow, blue, black
☐ Strip of green felt 10in long by 1½in wide
☐ White buttonhole twist thread
☐ Kapok or washable stuffing
☐ Glue
☐ Tracing paper

Cutting out

Trace the pattern, including all join marks, and pin the tracing paper pattern to one piece of white felt, positioning the pieces as indicated on the layout plan below. Cut out all the pieces, cutting on the line. Unpin the pattern and pin it to the second piece of white felt and cut out the pieces as before. Indicate all the join marks on the wrong side of the felt in pencil. Mark ear and eye positions on the right side with basting stitches.
Cut out the collar and flowers.

Making the lamb

Place the two body pieces together, wrong sides facing, pin and baste. Using double thread, sew around the head from points A to C in blanket stitch. The stitches should be deep enough to hold the felt firmly together. Stuff the head firmly with kapok, pushing the stuffing in with the eraser end of a pencil. Sew around the tail from point D to B and stuff with kapok. Join the two inside leg pieces together along the edges E to F. Sew the inside legs section to the main body, matching A to E and B to F (see diagram).
Stuff the legs firmly and then the body, through the gap left open in the back (C to D), and sew up the gap.

Finishing and trimming

Using a single thread, sew each pair of ear pieces together, and then sew the completed ears to the head along the marks G to H using buttonhole stitch.
Glue the black pupils to the pale blue eyes and secure with stitches all around. Glue the completed eye to each side of the head. Sew around each eye in buttonhole stitch. Embroider the eyebrows in black thread.

Making the garland
Roll up the cut-out flower pieces and secure at the base with a few stitches. Wrap another flower piece in a contrasting color around the roll and stitch to secure.
Fold the strip of green felt lengthwise and join the long edges with blanket stitch. Sew each flower very firmly to the green strip. Join the ends, and place the garland around the lamb's neck.

Pattern pieces for a lamb 9½in high. Cut two of each piece ►
▼ *Layout plan for lamb pieces and flowers* ▼ *Inside leg sewn to the main body*

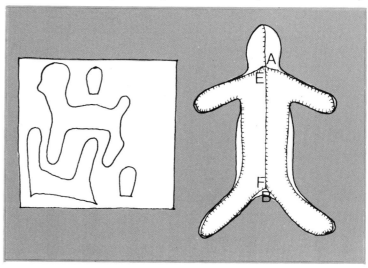

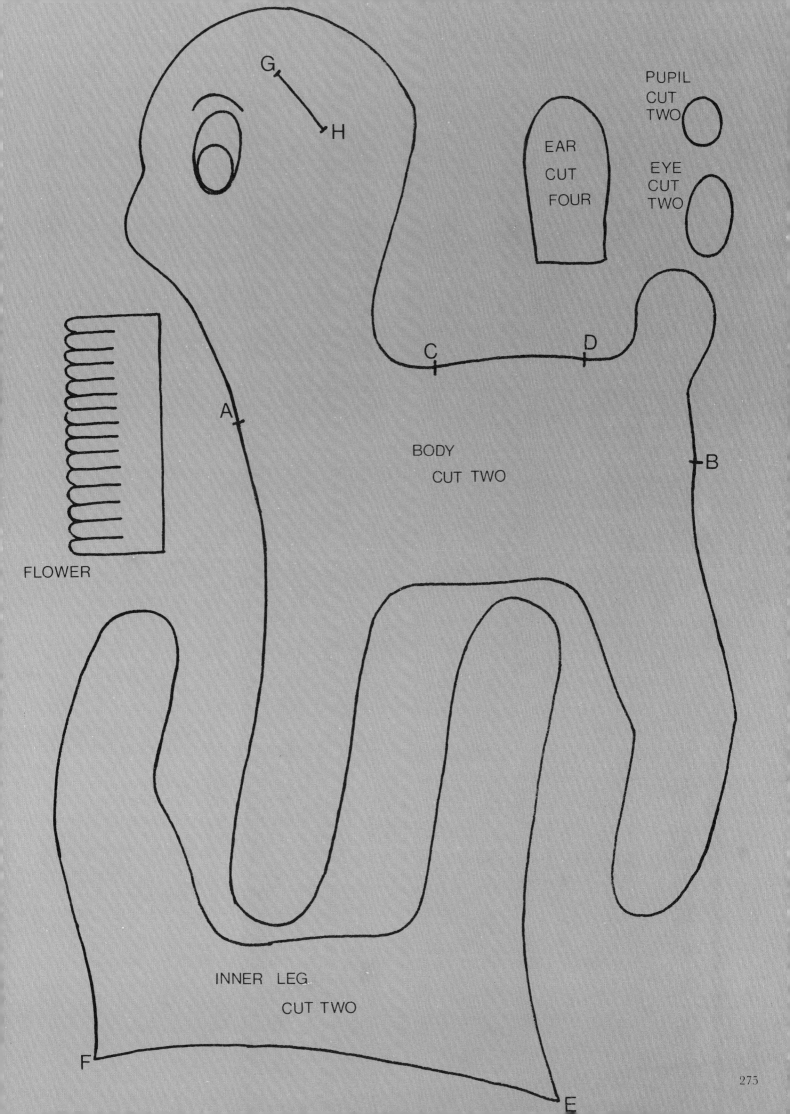

G

H

PUPIL
CUT
TWO

EAR
CUT
FOUR

EYE
CUT
TWO

C

D

A

BODY

CUT TWO

B

FLOWER

INNER LEG

CUT TWO

F

E

275

One pattern - many skirts

Knee-length, midi or long, gored or dirndl—which is right for you? Here you see how easy it is to experiment by altering the basic skirt pattern from Dressmaking chapter 4, page 76. It is transformed into a four-gore skirt in a choice of lengths, and a dirndl. There is a pleated variation in the next chapter. Once you have mastered these styles, you can try adapting the pattern even more yourself.

The four-gore skirt

The stages for making this skirt are the same as for the simple flared skirt in Dressmaking chapters 4 to 7, pages 76, 79, 116, and 136, except that you allow for, and stitch, a center front and center back seam.

Fabric requirements
54in width—for sizes $34\frac{1}{2}$ to 42in hip, your skirt length plus 8 inches. For size 44in hip, allow $\frac{1}{4}$yd extra.
36in width—for all sizes ($34\frac{1}{2}$ to 44in hip), twice your skirt length plus 11 inches.
Remember to buy a 7in skirt zipper and matching thread; also, hooks and eyes, seam binding and belting or stiffening for the waistband.

Layout for 54in wide fabric, $34\frac{1}{2}$in to 36in hip

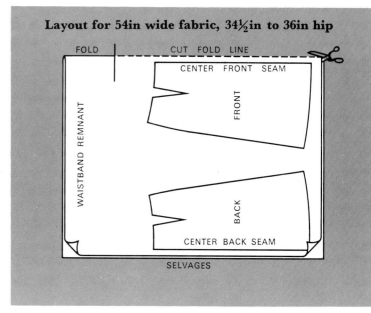

Layout for 54in wide fabric, 38in to 42in hip

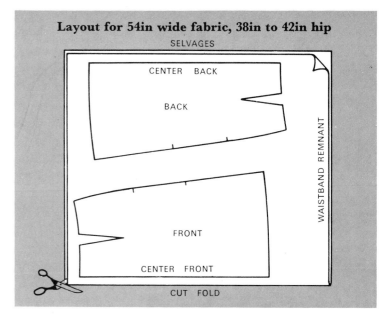

Layout for 36in wide fabric, for all hip sizes

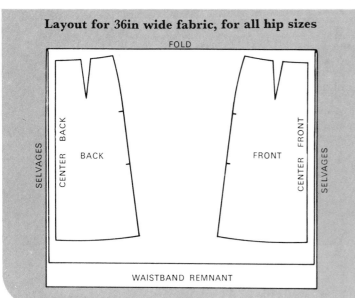

Layout for 54in wide fabric, 44in hip

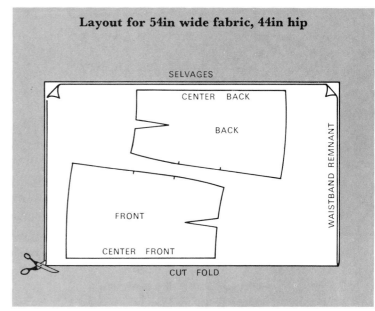

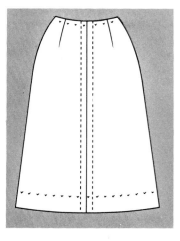

Layout and cutting

Using the basic flared skirt pattern from Dressmaking chapter 4, pg. 76, select the correct layout for your size and fabric width (see diagrams opposite). Remember that the center front and center back seams should always be cut on the straight grain of the fabric. Before you cut out the skirt, cut the fold to the length of the paper pattern. This will help you to remember to leave an allowance for the center front seam when you are cutting out the pattern pieces.

Making the skirt

Mark around the pattern with tailor's tacks. Add $\frac{3}{4}$in seam and $2\frac{1}{2}$in hem allowances all around. Then follow the basting, fitting, stitching and finishing instructions given for the simple flared skirt, with the addition of a center front and center back seam.

Topstitching

If you want to give the center front and center back seams added importance, topstitch them before you put on the waistband and sew up the hem. Using a slightly thicker machine twist to make the stitches stand out from the fabric, run a parallel row of stitching $\frac{3}{8}$in from the seam, on each side of it. You can also work topstitching by hand, using a $\frac{1}{4}$in running stitch.

Three different looks from the basic flared skirt pattern. Just adapt the length and choose a suitable fabric for any occasion ▶

The dirndl skirt

There isn't an easier skirt to make than the gathered dirndl. You can make it from a strip of fabric about 1¼ times your hip measurement or, if the fabric is fine enough, you can use more for greater fullness. But to take the guesswork out of making this skirt, use the pattern for the basic flared skirt given in Dressmaking chapter 4, page 76, as a guide.

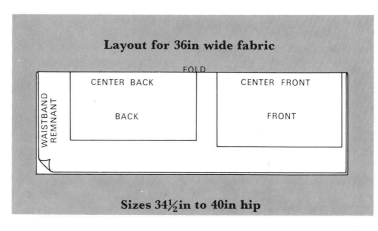

Fabric requirements
54in width—for all sizes (34½ to 44in hip), your skirt length plus 7 inches.
36in width—for all sizes (34½ to 44in hip), twice your skirt length plus 11 inches.
N.B. This style is only flattering to sizes over 38in hip if the waist is small and neat.
You will also need a 7in zipper, ½in wide straight seam binding and matching thread. Remember to buy hooks and eyes and belting or stiffening, if necessary, for the waistband.

How to prepare the pattern
Preparing the pattern is simple. To obtain the fullness required for the gathers, just lay the basic pattern on a sheet of paper and square it off as the diagram opposite shows.
Remove the basic pattern from the paper and mark the skirt sections, back and front.

Layout and cutting
After selecting the correct layout for your size and fabric width, place the squared-off pattern pieces on the fold of the fabric as indicated in the diagrams on this page, mark around them and mark the center lines on the skirt.
Cut out the fabric, remembering to add ¾in seam allowances and 2½in hem allowances.

Making the skirt
Stitch the side seams and insert the zipper.
Make a row of stitches for gathering the waist on each side of the waist seam, ¼in apart, on the right side of your skirt. It is important to stitch on the right side of the fabric because you must always pull up gathers from the wrong side.
When stitching the gathering stitches, use the longest stitch setting on the sewing machine and slacken off the upper tension. This will make it easier for you to draw the threads of the lower stitches into gathers later.

The waist stay
Before you gather the waistline of the skirt, first prepare a stay tape or a waist guide.
Cut a length of ½in seam binding the length of your waist plus 1in for ease.
Mark this strip by measuring against the original basic pattern as follows. Starting with the left end of the tape, measure off the back section of the basic pattern from side seam to center (excluding the width of the darts). Mark this measurement on the tape with basting thread. This mark will be the center back. From this mark, measure off the same amount again to find the position of the opposite side seam.

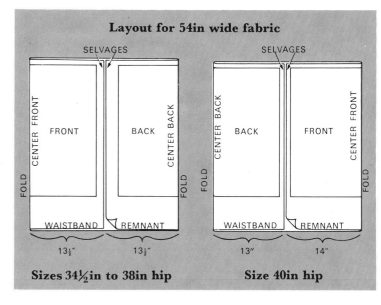

Then, using the front section of the basic pattern and starting from the opposite end of the tape, measure and mark from side seam to the center front and from the center front to side seam as before.
When you have finished marking the tape, pin it to the side seam and center marks on the skirt.

Preparing the waist seam for the waistband
Pull up the gathers by picking up the thread ends of the two rows of machine stitches and gently ease the fullness into even gathers along the waistline between the pins.
Pin on the seam binding, placing the pins at right angles to the waistline, then baste and stitch the tape to the skirt (see diagram at top of opposite page).

Notes on stitching gathers
When you are stitching gathers to a straight piece of fabric, always make sure the gathers are uppermost. If you leave them out of sight, under the tape or other straight fabric, you'll find there is a tendency for them to get caught up into the seam.
As you are not able to hold them out of the way of the machine needle, the gathers are likely to tilt and bunch, and the finished result will be bulky and uneven.
If, sometimes, you cannot avoid leaving gathers out of sight or under the work, make a row of basting stitches on each side of the seamline, to prevent them from moving.
Now that you've prepared the waist seam, you are ready to stitch on the waistband.

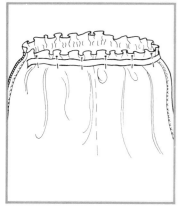
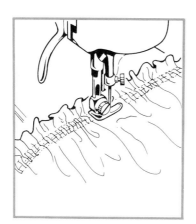

▲ *Waist stay pinned into position*   ▲ *Stitching gathers over waist stay*
▼ *How to prepare the pattern for the dirndl by adapting the basic skirt*

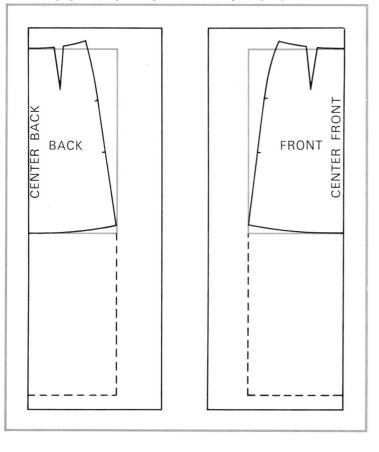

You can use any of the waist finishes (except the invisible waist-band) given in Dressmaking chapters 7 and 8, pages 136 and 156, for the dirndl skirt because the waistbands are attached by using center markings. This means that, regardless of the position of the seams in relation to the waistband, provided you always make the center marking on the skirt opposite the opening and match this to the center marking on the waistband, you can put the zipper where you like, in the side seam, the center back, or center front seam.

Evening dirndl

The dirndl is an ideal style to make up as a long evening skirt and preparing the pattern is, again, very simple. Measure the side length from waist to floor. When doing so, be sure to put on the shoes you will be wearing with the finished skirt, because a high heel can take up as much as 3 or 4 inches. Then, all you need to do is to add the extra length to the pattern by extending it from the hem, indicated by the dotted lines in the diagram above.

Sleeping pretty

Give a beautiful satin nightie a touch of luxury with a dreamy spray of hydrangeas. Add a few to accent a pretty yoke, neat waist or even a pajama pocket—and you can always spare a spray to match for the corner of your sheets or pillow cases. Trace the design straight from this page and transfer it onto the material.

If you are embroidering a ready-made garment, it is easiest if you select a smooth flat area to work on. But if you're making your own lingerie you can embroider the cut pieces before putting them together.

Work smooth satin stitch flowers in pure silk yarn, with rougher, textured leaves in six-strand floss. Or, for contrast, you may want to outline some of the flowers with line stitches using French knots for centers or perhaps appliqué the leaves. Thread colors will depend on the background color. Choose a pale hydrangea blue, or deep violet on white, apricot on pale pink or an inky blue on a pale blue nightie.

Pattern Library

Strawberries and toadstools

This charming ring of toadstools decorates a tablecloth, but a single group of them would brighten the bodice of a little girl's dress, a pocket or a potholder.

To make the circle of motifs shown here, first buy or make a circular tablecloth. Fold it in half twice to find the center, then anchor a thread with a pin to the center, tie a piece of tailor's chalk to the other end and draw a circle as a guide for transferring the design. Divide the circumference of this circle into eight by folding the cloth in half three times through the center and mark the division with lines of basting. Trace the toadstools from the illustration on this page and enlarge them to the size you want (see Embroidery chapter 15). Arrange the motifs around the drawn circle, then transfer them onto the cloth, repeating whichever groups you wish.

Suggested stitches for embroidering the toadstools and strawberries: long and short stitch. Leaves: satin stitch and long and short stitch. Stems: outline stitch. Spots on toadstool caps and berries: French knots or seeding.

Rose-embroidered baby bootees

Bootees are fun to make, and why not embroider them? The rosebud here could be applied to any baby's clothes or around the neck or cuffs of an older child's blouse.

Size

Directions are for size birth to 3 months.

Gauge

Yarn is used double throughout, giving a gauge of 4sts and 4 rows to 1in over st st worked on No.5 needles.

Knitting Know-how 15

Materials

1oz 3-ply baby yarn
One pair No.5 needles or Canadian No.8
No.F (4.00 mm.) crochet hook
Embroidery yarns or cotton

N.B. Every knitting leaflet uses different abbreviations. For example, 'K up 1', used here, is an alternative abbreviation for 'M1K', and the working method is the same. 'P up 1' is an alternative for 'M1P'.

Bootees

Using No.5 needles and double yarn, cast on 33sts for center

of the sole of the bootee.
1st row K.
2nd row K1, K up 1, K15, K up 1, K1, K up 1, K15, K up 1, K1.
3rd row K.
4th row K1, K up 1, K17, K up 1, K1, K up 1, K17, K up 1, K1.
5th row K.
6th row K1, K up 1, K19, K up 1, K1, K up 1, K19, K up 1, K1.
7th-15th rows K.
Next row K25. Turn.
Begin working center front as follows:
1st row Sl 1, P5. Turn.
2nd row Sl 1, K6. Turn.
3rd row Sl 1, P7. Turn.
4th row Sl 1, K8. Turn.
5th row Sl 1, P9. Turn.
6th row K28.
7th row P28, P2 tog. Turn.
8th row K9, K2 tog. Turn.
9th row P10, P2 tog. Turn.
10th row K10, K2 tog. Turn.
11th row P10, P2 tog. Turn.
12th row K10, K2 tog. Turn.
13th row P10, P2 tog, P to end of row.
14th row K22, K2 tog, K to end of row.
15th row P to end. 37sts.

16th row K1, *ytf, K2 tog, rep from * to end.
17th row P.
Work 7 rows K1, P1 rib.
Next row K1, *ytf, sl 1, ytb, K1, rep from * to end.
Next row Sl 1, *ytf, K1, ytb, sl 1, rep from * to end.
Next row K1, *ytf, sl 1, ytb, K1, rep from * to end.
Work invisible binding off—see Knitting Know-how, chapter 6.

Finishing

Join back and sole seam. Work a crochet chain about 14in long or use ribbon. Thread through eyelets, then attach crochet rosettes. Embroider rosebud motif on bootee, following the 6 steps illustrated below.

To work a crochet rosette

Ch7.
Into 2nd ch from hook work 5dc, *5dc into next ch, rep from * to end. Fasten off. This will curl around to form a rosette. Secure ends through center and sew one rosette to either end of chain.

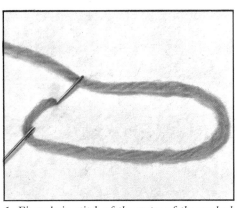

1. First chain stitch of the center of the rosebud

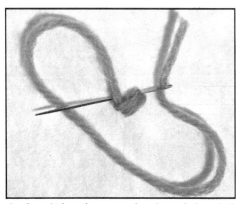

2. Completing the center in close chain stitch

3. Working the outer rings, still in chain stitch

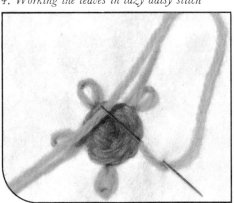

4. Working the leaves in lazy daisy stitch

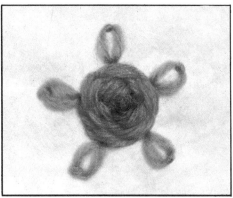

5. The completed rosebud and its leaves

6. The rosebud embroidered on the bootee

Make mine mobile

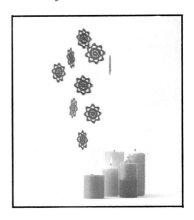

Two motifs with many uses —Make them in miniature, using fine cotton and hook, for a choker or a mobile; in heavy yarn for a belt; in cotton for a cocktail mat.

Star flower motif

With center color, ch8. Join into a circle with ss into first ch.
1st round. Using same color ch3, then work 31dc into circle. Join with ss into 3rd of first 3ch. Break yarn and leave the end for darning in.
2nd round. Join contrast with ss into top of last st, ch2, work 1dc into each of next 3dc leaving last loop of each dc on hook (4 loops on hook), yoh, draw through all 4 loops to form cluster, ch4, *work 1dc into each of next 4dc leaving last loop of each dc on hook (5 loops on hook), yoh, draw through all loops to form cluster, ch4, rep from * 6 times. Join with ss into top of first cluster.
3rd round. Work 1sc, 1hdc, 1dc, 1tr all into first ch4 space, ch5, *work 1ss, 1sc, 1hdc, 1dc, 1tr all into next ch4 space, ch5, rep from * 6 times.

Join with ss into first st.
4th round. Work 1sc into sc of preceding round, 1hdc into next hdc, 1dc into next dc, 1tr into next tr, ch7, *1ss into next ss, 1sc into next sc, 1hdc into next hdc, 1dc into dc, 1tr into tr, ch7, rep from * 6 times. Join with ss into first st. Break yarn, darn in all ends.

Lace star motif

Ch6. Join into a circle with ss into first ch.
1st round. Ch5, *1dc into circle, ch2, rep from * 6 times. Join with ss to 4th of first 5ch.
2nd round. Ch3, work 3dc into first space omitting last step of each dc so that 4 loops rem on hook after working 3rd dc, yoh and draw through all loops, ch5, *work dc into next space leaving last loop of each dc unworked on hook (5 loops when 4th dc is worked), yoh and draw through all loops, ch5, rep from * 6 times. Join with ss into 3rd of first 3ch.
3rd round. *Ch3, work 1dc, ch5, 1dc all into 3rd of first 5ch of preceding round, ch3,

1sc into top of next cluster of preceding round, rep from * 7 times. Join with ss into first ch.
4th round. Ch1, 2sc into first ch3 space, 5sc into next ch5 space, 3sc into next ch3 space, *3sc into next ch3 space, 5sc into next ch5 space, 3sc into next ch3 space, rep from * 6 times. Join with ss into first ch. Break yarn and darn all ends invisibly into work.

Make a mobile with the starry motifs shown here (spray with non-inflammable lacquer to stiffen them). If you hang it near a very gentle heat, like a candle flame, the stars will always be on the move.▼

▼ *Star flower motif*

▼ *Lace star motif*

The prettiest suit in town (part 1)

The directions given here are for the crochet suit jacket and buttons. You will find the skirt and blouse to complete the suit in the next Basic Wardrobe chapter.

Sizes

Jacket: directions are for 32in bust.
The figures in brackets [] refer to the 34 and 36in sizes respectively.
Length, 22[22½:22½]in.
Sleeve seam, 12½in.

> ### Gauge
> 6½sts and 4¾ rows to 1in over patt worked on No.C crochet hook

Materials

Reynolds Parfait, 30 gr ball
Jacket: 18 [20:22] balls in main color, A
1 ball in contrast, B
Skirt: 17[18:20] balls in main color, A
1 ball in contrast, B
Blouse: 13[15:17] balls in contrast, B
Eighteen small button molds
One No. C (2.50 mm.) crochet hook
One No. B (2.00 mm.) crochet hook

Jacket back

Using No.C crochet hook and A, ch111[119:127].
1st row (right side) 1sc into 2nd ch from hook, *1sc into next ch, rep from * to end of row.
110[118:126] sts.
2nd row Ch3, skip first st, *(yoh, draw loop through next st, yoh, draw loop through 2 loops on hook) twice, yoh, draw loop through
284

all 3 loops on hook, ch1, rep from * ending with 1dc in last st. Turn.
3rd row 2sc in first ch sp, *2sc in next ch sp, rep from * ending with 2sc in 3 turning ch sp. Turn.
The 2nd and 3rd rows form the patt and are rep throughout.
Continue in patt until back measures 13½in, ending with a 2nd patt row.

Shape raglan
1st row Ss to 2nd ch sp, 2sc in this ch sp, patt to last ch sp. Turn.
106[114:122] sts.
2nd row Patt. Turn.
3rd row 1sc in each of first 2 ch sp, patt to last 2 ch sp, 1sc in each of last 2 ch sp, thus dec 2sts at each end of row. Turn.
Rep 2nd and 3rd rows until 34[34:38] sts rem.
Work 1 row. Fasten off.

Right front

Using No.C crochet hook and A, ch45[49:53].
Work 1st and 2nd rows as given for back. 44[48:52] sts. **

Shape front
1st row (3rd patt row) Ch3, 1sc into 2nd ch from hook, 1sc in next ch, patt to end. Turn. 46[50:54] sts.
2nd row Patt. Turn.
3rd-6th rows Rep 1st and 2nd rows twice. 50[54:58] sts.
7th row As 1st row.
8th-10th rows Patt.
11th-14th rows As 7th-10th rows.
15th-16th rows As 1st and

2nd rows. 56[60:64] sts.
Continue in patt without shaping until front measures same length as back to raglan shaping, ending with a 2nd patt row (front edge).

Shape raglan
1st row Patt to last ch sp. Turn. 54[58:62] sts.
2nd row Patt. Turn.
3rd row Patt to last 2 ch sp, 1sc in each of last 2 ch sp to dec 2sts at raglan edge. Turn.
Rep 2nd and 3rd rows until 30[32:34] sts rem, ending at front edge.

Shape neck
Next row Ss to 6th ch sp, 2sc in this ch sp, patt to last 2 ch sp, 1sc in each of last 2 ch sp. Turn. 18[20:22] sts.
Next row Patt. Turn.
Next row 1sc in each of first 2 ch sp, patt to last 2 ch sp, 1sc in each of last 2 ch sp. Turn.
Rep last 2 rows 2[2:3] times more. 6[8:6] sts.
Now keep neck edge straight and dec only at raglan edge as before, until 2sts rem.
Work 1 row. Fasten off.

Left front

Work as given for right front, to **

Shape front
1st row Patt. Turn.
2nd row Ch5, working into 5th ch from hook, patt to end. Turn. 46[50:54] sts.
3rd-6th rows As 1st and 2nd rows, twice. 50[54:58] sts.
Work to correspond to right front, reversing all shaping.

Right sleeve

Using No.C crochet hook and A, ch37[39:41] and work 8 rows in patt. 36[38:40] sts.
Inc row Work 3sc in each of first 2 ch sp, patt to end. 38[40:42] sts. Work 9 rows without shaping. Break yarn.
Using No.C crochet hook and A, ch27[29:31].
Work 8 rows in patt. 26[28:30] sts.

Inc row Patt to last 2 ch sp, 3sc in each of last 2 ch sp. 28[30:32] sts.
Work 10 rows without shaping. Do not turn, but continue in patt across 38[40:42] sts on first piece. 66[70:74] sts. Work 1 row.
Inc 2sts as before at each end of next and every following 12th row until there are 78[82:86] sts.
Work without shaping until 12in from beg, ending with a 2nd patt row.

Shape cap
1st row Ss to 2nd ch sp, 2sc in this ch sp, patt to last ch sp. Turn.
2nd-4th rows Patt.
5th row 1sc in each of first 2 ch sp, patt to last 2 ch sp, 1sc in each of last 2 ch sp. Turn.
Rep last 4 rows 0[1:1] times more, then rep 4th and 5th rows until 6sts rem.
Work 1 row. Fasten off.

Left sleeve

Work as for right sleeve, noting that first piece to be worked will be the small piece.

Finishing

Block and press each piece on wrong side using a warm iron and damp cloth.
Sew sleeve seams.

Sleeve borders

Right sleeve
Using No.B crochet hook and B, with RS facing, beg at top of slit and work 1 row sc down slit and along lower edge.
Work 3 rows sc, working extra sc at corner to keep it square.
Next row Work in sc, making 3 button loops evenly spaced down slit. To work a button loop, ch6 and skip 2sts. Work along lower edge and up other side of slit. Turn.
Work picot edge
Next row 1ss in first st, *1ss in next st, ch3, 1ss in

same st, 1ss in next st, rep from * down slit, along lower edge and up top of slit, working picots along ch of button loops. Fasten off. Overlap button edge and stitch on RS at top of slit.

Left sleeve

Work as for right sleeve. **N.B.** Button loops will be worked at opposite end of row. Using a flat seam, join raglan and side seams.

Work front border

Beg at side seam on right front. Using No.B crochet hook and B, with RS facing, work 1 row sc along lower edge of right front, around corner and up right front edge, around neck, down left front and along edge to beg. Turn. Work 3 more rows sc, working extra sc around curves and at neck edge.

Next row Work in sc, making 12 button loops as on sleeve, evenly spaced up right edge, the first to come $\frac{1}{2}$in in from where curve ends, the 12th to come 2sts down from neck edge. Work to end in sc. Turn.

Work picot edge as for sleeves all around. Fasten off.

Button covers

Using No.B crochet hook and B, ch4. Join into circle with ss into first ch. **1st row** Work 9sc into circle. Work 4 rounds sc. Fasten off. (Work eighteen.)

Place button molds inside covers and draw up tightly. Stitch in position. Press seams.

▼ *Detail of jacket buttonhole edges*

Enlarging and reducing designs

Embroidery 15

What you will need:
- ☐ Tracing paper
- ☐ Graph or squared paper
- ☐ Ruler
- ☐ Fine felt-tipped pen
- ☐ Soft pencil and eraser
- ☐ Carbon paper (optional)

Whether you create your own embroidery designs or adapt those you find in books or magazines, it is useful to know how to alter the size. With the method of enlarging or reducing explained in this chapter, you will no longer have to worry if the initial design is miniature or enormous—you will be able to alter it to the exact size you want. You will be surprised to find how easy it is to enlarge or reduce designs.

Method

1. First trace the outline of the design onto tracing paper.

2. Carefully transfer tracing to graph or small-squared paper.

3. Draw a rectangle around the tracing.

4. Draw a diagonal through the rectangle. Extend two adjacent sides of the rectangle to the final size you want, then draw lines at right angles from the ends of the extended sides to meet at the diagonal. If it confuses you to have the rectangles inside one another, draw the larger to one side of the smaller one.

5. Count the total number of squares in the small rectangle and divide the largest rectangle into the same number of squares to form a grid. Draw this in pen as you may want to erase and re-draw some of the lines of the design to improve its shape. Now in pencil carefully copy this design onto the larger grid. It will help if you make tiny marks on each square where the lines of the design cross it, then you can join up these marks.

To reduce a design, use the same method in reverse.

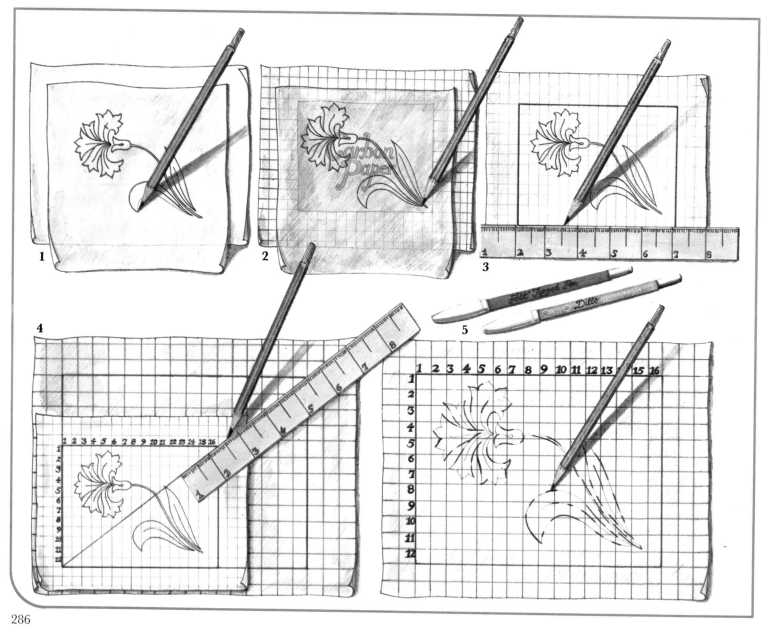

286

Hot water bottle cover

This pretty hot water bottle cover has an elegant carnation appliqué motif in subtle tones of blue and green. Make it in any color you wish, using either tones of the same color or bright contrasting colors. Of course you need not use the design for appliqué; the motif can be worked in long and short stitch, satin stitch, or just as an outline using simple chain stitch or one of the chain stitch variations.

Materials you will need:

- ☐ ½yd 36in wide material
- ☐ ½yd 36in wide fleecy lining
- ☐ Scraps of material in blue and green (all washable)
- ☐ 6-strand embroidery floss in blue and green
- ☐ ¾yd nylon velvet ribbon
- ☐ Sewing thread

Instructions for making the cover

Enlarge both the pattern for the cover and the motif to the required size. Cut two pattern pieces for the outside of the cover and two pieces for the lining, allowing ⅝in seam allowances on all edges. Mark the stitching line all around each section with a line of basting. Transfer the design, following the instructions given in Embroidery chapter 4, page 68, onto either one or both sides of the cover.

Transfer the flower and leaf shapes onto the contrasting materials and cut them out. Place the shapes on the cover and baste them in place. Stitch down the shapes either with a line of zigzag machine stitches, or by hand with buttonhole stitch using 3 strands of embroidery cotton. Embroider the details on the flower and leaf sections in outline stitch with 2 strands of embroidery cotton, and the stem in overcast stitch. When the appliqué and embroidery are complete, press the cover pieces.

Line cover pieces separately. Place linings to covers right sides facing, baste and stitch around edges C-C over top and A-A around base, being careful to follow curves to maintain a good shape. Trim away seam allowances to ¼in, clip into corners at points A and B and cut notches on the curves. (Always cut notches away from the seamline to avoid cutting into the seam.) Turn covers to the outside and, with the right sides facing you, baste the stitched edges, easing the curves into shape.

Place right sides of covers together and stitch from A-C on both sides. Press seams open. Turn back seam allowance on lining to stitching line and slip stitch in place. Turn lined cover right sides out, press edges and remove basting. Sew ribbon securely to the center back of the cover and trim the ends to tie in a bow.

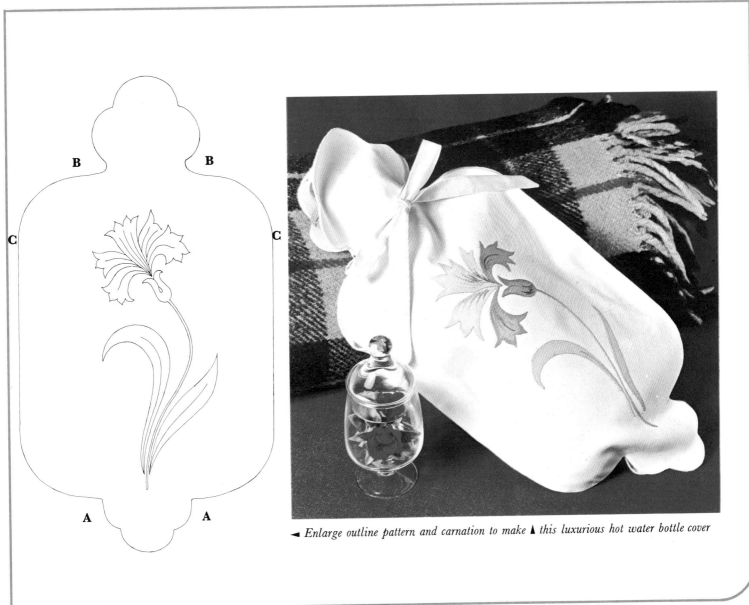

◄ *Enlarge outline pattern and carnation to make* ▲ *this luxurious hot water bottle cover*

Collector's pillows

Home Sewing 2

This chapter on Home Sewing shows you how to liven up your living room by making a collection of pretty pillows. Pillows not only make sinking into chairs and sofas more enjoyable, but they also add decorative shapes and striking patches of color to the general scheme of any room. Follow these easy instructions for making a simple corded pillow cover, with hints on the most suitable fillings. Once you have mastered the basic technique, you can then tackle more adventurous designs. The pillows shown below are made using patchwork, machine embroidery, crochet and needlepoint.

It's the filling that counts

What goes inside a pillow is quite as important as its covering. There are several types of filling—feathers-and-down make the most luxurious, but many people now use a Dacron fiber as this is washable. Kapok is cheaper, but tends to go lumpy after a while. Foam pads are unwelcoming to lean against and eventually curl at the edges. Many pillow departments now have a large selection of round and square pillow forms in all sizes with a choice of fillings, which you can cover as you choose.

If you plan to make your own pillow forms, you can buy Dacron fiber, kapok or several qualities in feathers-and-down by the bag. But, if you are using feathers, remember to make the bag in a down-proof fabric. For Dacron or kapok fillings, a fine fabric such as sateen would be very suitable.

Simple corded pillow cover

Materials for a pillow 18in by 18in

☐ 37in of 36in wide fabric (a bare yard means skimping), or 18½in of 48in wide fabric
   With large-pattern fabrics allow enough extra to center the design on both sides of the pillow.
☐ 2¼yds of cording
☐ 12in zipper

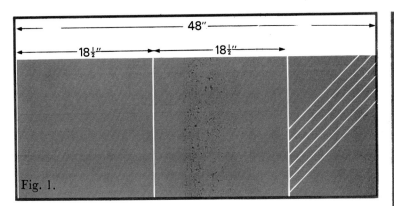

Fig. 1.

Making the pillow cover

To make a cover fit neatly, you should make it half an inch smaller all around than the actual pillow size.

Cut out the cover as in the diagram for either 36in (Fig. 2) or 48in (Fig. 1) wide fabric. Join the bias strips for covering the cording and baste the covered cord around the right side of the pillow top.

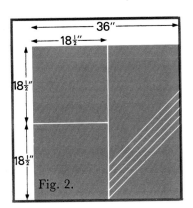

Fig. 2.

Clip the outside edges of the bias strip at the corners of the pillow and trim away the fabric so that it lies flat (Fig. 3). Baste half the zipper (wrong side uppermost) to the center of one side of the pillow top. Using the zipper foot on your sewing machine, stitch all around the pillow top as close to the cording as possible (Fig. 4).

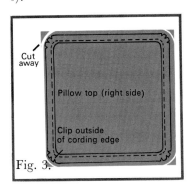

Cut away

Pillow top (right side)

Clip outside of cording edge

Fig. 3.

Zipper (wrong side uppermost)

Top (right side)

Fig. 4.

Now baste the other half of the zipper (again wrong side uppermost) to the back of the pillow, and stitch (Fig. 5). With right sides facing, baste the two halves of the pillow together and stitch along the stitchline for the cording.

Overcast the raw edges and finish off the two ends of the zipper. Press cover with a hot iron and turn it right side out. The sketch below shows how the corded pillow will look when it is finished (Fig. 6).

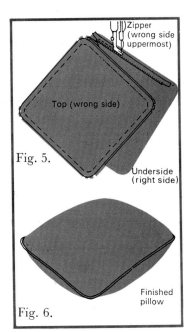

Zipper (wrong side uppermost)

Top (wrong side)

Fig. 5.

Underside (right side)

Finished pillow

Fig. 6.

These simple scatter pillows show lots of design ideas for you to copy and which may inspire you to develop ideas of your own. They are all of different shapes and sizes and incorporate techniques such as patchwork, embroidery, appliqué, knitting and fringing. Use pillows to make a hard chair more comfortable, to disguise a day-bed during the day or to brighten dark or plain upholstery. You can also use pillows to unite a color scheme. For example, use left-overs of drapery material when making your pillows and you will find that the overall look of the room will hold together far better.

Collector's Piece

A Danish rose

Cross-stitch is one of the
oldest forms of embroidery.
For centuries it has been
used in traditional
European folk and peasant
embroideries to decorate
national costumes and
household articles.
Each country has developed
its own particular style to
such an extent that it is
possible to determine where
a particular piece of work
or design originated. For
instance, modern Danish
cross-stitch designs usually
depict forms in a very
realistic manner. The rounded
shapes of flowers, birds and
animals are embroidered in
delicate, pretty colors in
carefully selected tones
which, when worked together,
enhance this realistic effect.
This delightful rose motif
is typical of the Danish style
in cross-stitch, and can be
used in many exciting ways.
Here it is shown worked in
two ways to create completely
contrasting effects. One rose
is worked in chunky yarns
on canvas, the other in
stranded floss on fine linen
and mounted in a tiny gold
frame.
Worked on linen with 24
threads to 1in over 2 threads
each way, the rose will
measure about $2\frac{1}{2}$in by $2\frac{1}{2}$in.
Worked as a cushion, the
same motif measures about
$7\frac{1}{2}$in by $7\frac{1}{2}$in—the different
scale is achieved by working
the cross-stitch over 3 threads
each way on single-weave
canvas with 12 threads to
1in, using 2 strands of knitting
worsted throughout.

Enmeshed in stitches

Despite its light and gauzy appearance, tulle is very hard-wearing. It consists of threads woven into hexagonal holes and the fabric makes an ideal background for embroidery for wedding veils, christening robes and lingerie.

There are two types of embroidery on tulle—each with its own working technique. The simplest is worked free style, without a pattern, on a coarse meshed tulle. The other looks rather like lace, the embroidery stitches being worked within a stitched outline on a tulle of finer mesh.

Simple geometric shapes and straightforward patterns are usually worked on the coarser meshes. For complicated designs on finer meshes, it is better to use a pattern.

Materials for embroidery
Tulle is sold in varying widths up to 144 inches wide and is made of nylon, and more rarely, of silk. Both are suitable for embroidery. The thread used for embroidery on tulle should be soft and run through the meshes easily without breaking them. Pearl cotton No.3 or No.5 is suitable for coarse meshed tulle and No.8 or No.12 for finer meshes.

Preparing a pattern
Preparation of tulle for embroidery is very important. The chosen design is copied onto tracing paper, the tulle placed upon it and a piece of firm cardboard placed under the paper. Baste the three layers together so that the design can be seen through the tulle and the cardboard supports the tulle for easy working.

For large areas of embroidery, such as a wedding veil, architect's linen should be used. The design is copied onto the linen and the tulle basted to it.

The needle used should be blunt, such as a tapestry needle, and in proportion to the mesh.

Working method
The outline of the design can be worked in any of the stitches illustrated in this chapter and some of them are also used for filling the pattern. To begin working, run the needle through the mesh, according to whichever stitch is chosen, leaving the end of the thread loose (about 3 inches). After the embroidery work has been completed, darn the end into the back of the work so that it is invisible. Much of the effect of embroidery on tulle depends on even work, and care should be taken not to pucker the fabric.

Embroidering the mantilla
The mantilla illustrated is worked with simple stitches in white on black and would adapt for a bridal veil. The edge is buttonhole stitched, the motifs outlined in running stitch and filled with darning stitch. The flowers and leaves are joined with loose cording, and wavy stitch decorates the flower centers (see page 654).

▲ *An exotic embroidered mantilla*   ▼ *Detail of stitches on mantilla*

292

Running stitch
Pass the needle over one mesh of the tulle and under the next, alternately. Running stitch is used mostly for defining outlines, but it can also be worked as a filling.

Diagonal running stitch
Pick up every other mesh of the tulle, diagonally. To work this as a filling stitch, make several parallel rows up and down, skipping one row of holes between each stitched row, and using a thicker yarn.

Cording
First work a running stitch guide line, then overcast this as illustrated. This stitch is useful when you want a bolder line than the normal running stitch outline.

Outline stitch
This is worked in the same way as embroidery outline stitch on fabric. For each stitch pick up one mesh of the tulle, always keeping the yarn to the right or left of the needle, depending on the direction of the slope you are working.

Knife-pleated skirt

This smart knife-pleated skirt, which flatters any figure, is a variation of the basic skirt pattern which first appeared in Part 4.

Suitable fabrics

The fabric you use for a pleated skirt should be crease-resistant, but it should also be capable of taking a sharp crease under pressure and steam. Worsted woolens are particularly suitable; so are some acrylic fibers such as Orlon; polyester fibers such as Dacron and Trevira; linens, firmly woven wool tweeds and a number of mixed fiber fabrics.

Before buying any fabric, it's a good idea to ask if it will pleat well.

Fabric requirements

54in width—for all sizes ($34\frac{1}{2}$ to 44in hip), twice the skirt length plus 11 inches.

36in width—for all sizes ($34\frac{1}{2}$ to 44in hip), four times the skirt length plus 21 inches.

You will also need a 7in zipper and matching thread. Remember to buy hooks and eyes, seam binding and belting or other stiffening if you need them for the waistband.

Adapting the basic pattern

To begin, make a copy of the flared skirt pattern in Dressmaking chapter 4, page 76 to use as the basic pattern, but do not cut out the darts—just mark them in pencil.

Using the yardstick, extend the balance marks on the front and back right across the pattern pieces, as illustrated. The extended balance marks become meeting marks for the

pleats to insure that they will lie flat and hang well when stitched and pressed.

To obtain the cutting line on the pattern, measure the distance from the center front and center back lines to the lowest point of the dart. Measure and mark off this distance all the way down to the hem, making a series of pencil marks parallel to the center back and center front.

Connect these marks with a yardstick, taking the line through the center of the darts right up to the waistline, and down to the hem.

Now mark the pattern sections on each side of the new cutting lines, as front, side front, back, and side back. This will help you to avoid putting the wrong pieces together when you lay out the pattern.

Cut out the pattern pieces along the cutting lines.

Knife-pleated skirt in Trevira ►
▼ Front pattern, with cutting line

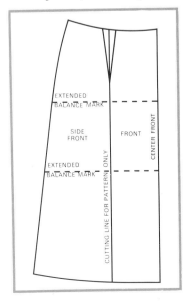

Layout for 54in wide fabric

Leave the fabric folded and lay it flat on the cutting table, allowing enough area to work on one complete section of the skirt at a time. Starting with the front section of the pattern, measure $2\frac{1}{2}$in from the fold and pin a line parallel to the length of the pattern pieces. Lay the center front line of the pattern along the pin line and pin the pattern down onto the fabric.

Then, measure 5in from the cutting line of the front section and mark the distance in the same way to the length of the pattern piece with a pin line.

Lay the cutting line of the side front section of the pattern along this pin line, securing the section with one or two pins so that it cannot move. Using the yardstick, lay it along the line of extended balance marks and make sure they go straight across both front and side front pattern pieces.

Now lay out the back skirt sections in the same way.

Make whatever adjustments are necessary to insure that the pattern sections line up correctly, and then pin them down securely onto the fabric.

Layout for 36in wide fabric

Open up the fabric to the full width and length on the cutting table. Fold in half so that the raw edges meet as shown in the layout diagram.

A point to watch—if you have bought a fabric with a nap, or a one-way design (this means the surface interest on the fabric goes in one direction, up or down), you must cut the length in half across the width, turn one layer and lay it in such a way that the surface interest runs in the same direction.

Before cutting, make sure the right sides of the cloth are facing each other—many a fine fabric has been spoiled by laying it out carelessly. Otherwise you will find after cutting that you have two right sides or two left sides and cannot match them up to make a whole garment.

When you lay out the front and back pattern sections, you must allow an extra $\frac{3}{4}$in for a seam on the fabric before you measure out the center line pleats. This is because the center front and center back are now on a selvage and not a fold as in the 54in width. Having done this, you can proceed in exactly the same way as described for the 54in layout.

To prepare for cutting

Now it is time to cut out the darts along the pencil lines (do not cut the fabric). Make sure that you curve them into the cutting line at the ends—don't let them finish on a sharp corner as this will make the pleat seam poke out at the end of the dart.

Tailor's tack around all the pattern pieces, remembering the balance marks on the pleat lines as well as on the side seams.

Mark out a $\frac{3}{4}$in seam allowance along the side seams and a $2\frac{1}{2}$in hem allowance.

When marking and cutting the seam allowance at the waist edge, more than the usual $\frac{3}{4}$in is needed. Therefore, do not follow the curve of the waistline, but take the normal seam allowance at the side seam and waistline point and then cut straight across to the center on both back and front. This gives you an extra $\frac{3}{4}$in seam allowance at the deepest point of the curve.

You will see when you have pleated the skirt that because of the curves of the side darts and waistline, extra seam allowance is needed to catch the right pleat at the front and left pleat at the back into the waistband.

Mark the normal waistline of the pattern on the fabric and leave the trimming of any excess seam allowance until after the skirt sections have been pleated.

After you have removed the pattern pieces, connect the balance marks with long lines of basting stitches.

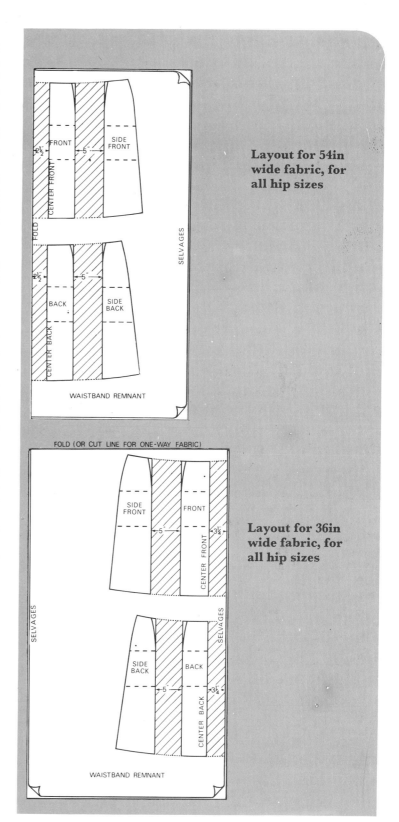

Layout for 54in wide fabric, for all hip sizes

Layout for 36in wide fabric, for all hip sizes

Pleating the skirt with soft pleats

Before you separate the layers of the skirt sections, you must first decide which way you are going to pleat the skirt.

One way is to lay the pleat lines together, baste them all the way down and then stitch them like a seam as far as the hipline, about 7in from the waist, and press the pleat to one side from the inside of the skirt. This sort of pleating will give the skirt a soft look. If you are going to do it this way, you'll have to mark a fold line between the pleat lines of the center front and side front sections, as shown in the illustration.

Pleating the skirt with tailored pleats

If you prefer a crisp, tailored look, lay the pleats from right to left on the outside of the skirt, matching the balance marks and basting them down securely along the edge.

Press them very lightly into position and topstitch about $\frac{1}{16}$in in from the edge, as far as the hipline.

Don't press the pleats in very sharply at this stage, but make up the skirt first.

When making the waistband, any of the methods in Dressmaking chapters 7, page 136 and 8, page 156 is suitable.

Special notes for finishing the pleated skirt

1. When you fit the skirt, do so with the pleats basted together. Turn back to the skirt fitting guide in Dressmaking chapter 6. When you have corrected the faults, fit the skirt again with the basting removed and pleats loose. They should hang straight and closed—not jutting forward or pulling open. If you see the pleats spreading, fan-like, toward the side seams, you will need to lift the skirt and pleats into the waist, until the pleats hang straight. If you see one pleat hanging badly, then this will need to be pulled up from the inside.

2. Before you stitch on the waistband, make sure the pleats are caught flat and firmly into the seam, then trim seam allowance.

3. If you've cut the skirt with a center front seam, refer to the side seam in the child's pleated skirt in Dressmaking chapter 13, page 256 for the hem finish. The easiest way to finish off the hem is to leave about two widths of the hem unstitched at the bottom of the seam in the pleat, turn up the hem, and then stitch through all layers to the bottom edge of the hem as shown below.

4. When turning up the hem, make hem at inner crease of the pleat about $\frac{1}{4}$in shorter, as below, to prevent pleats from showing.

5. Before you finally press in the pleats, make sure that you have removed all basting threads and tailor's tacks.

6. Sometimes pressing the thickness of pleats leaves impressions on the fabric which show on the right side. To remove these, carefully press under the pleats, on the wrong side.

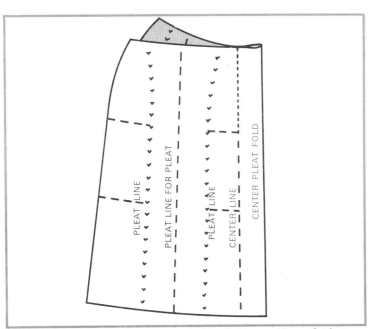

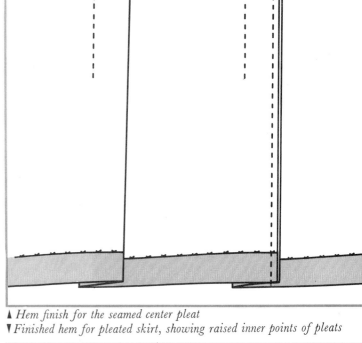

▲ *Pleating so that pleat lines meet on inside of skirt, making soft pleats*
▼ *Pleating from right to left on outside of skirt, making tailored pleats*

▲ *Hem finish for the seamed center pleat*
▼ *Finished hem for pleated skirt, showing raised inner points of pleats*

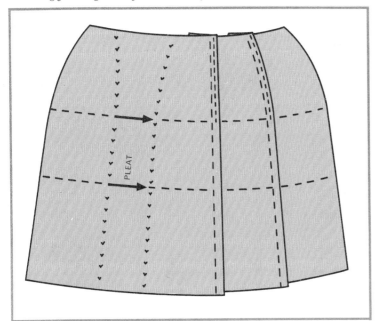

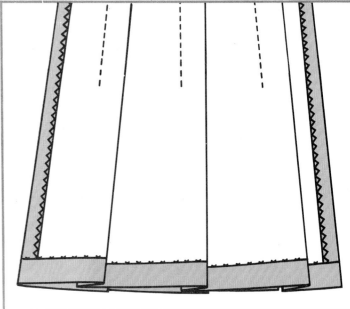

All about fabrics and fibers

Did you know that there are now pure wool tweeds and suede fabrics that you can pop safely into a washing machine? Or that men's jackets can be baked like hot potatoes in the oven to set their shape forever? Or that tweeds can now be knitted and that socks are being made with a permanently anti-odor finish?

Enormous advances have been made over the last twenty years in the textile industry by fiber and yarn manufacturers, weavers and knitters, who are continually developing better and better fabrics. This is all very well, but if the experts themselves can hardly keep up with all the new developments, how can the housewife find her way through the jungle of blends, weaves and finishes?

If you feel confused, don't worry. In this Take Care chapter, Creative Hands sets out the most up-to-date information, explains the variously-named man-made fibers, sorts out which fibers and blends are suitable for what, and examines the latest processes and finishes so that you know what to ask for when you go shopping.

It's important to know whether a fiber is man-made, natural, or a blend. In an increasingly time- and price-conscious world, man-mades have definite advantages. They are easy to care for and their quality and cost can be closely controlled. But no man-made fibers combine the best of the innate qualities of natural fibers.

For example, many man-mades are non-absorbent, which makes them inclined to be sticky and sweaty to wear, and they lack the thermal qualities which make the naturals warm in winter and cool in summer. Man-made fabrics also tend to create static electricity which attracts dirt. Very often the answer lies with

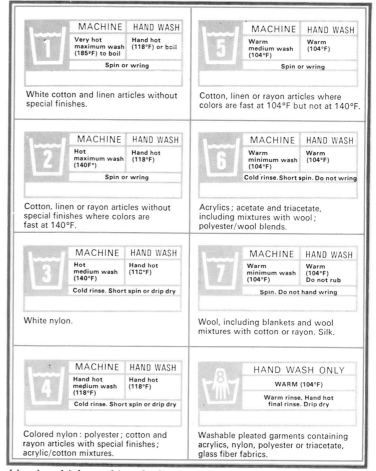

blends, which combine the best qualities of both natural and man-made fibers. (The cotton/polyester blends used for shirts combine the tough crease-resistance created by polyester with the cool comfort of cotton.)

The correct way to wash garments and household items depends on their fiber content. Natural fibers are easy to launder and will stand up to high temperatures, but man-made fibers require more careful handling. The chart above gives the instructions for the wash and care codes mentioned in this chapter.

To avoid disasters (left) and achieve successful results (right) follow the Creative Hands wash and care instructions given in this chapter

Natural fibers

	qualities	ways to wash
Cotton	*Cotton comes from the ripe, fluffy seedpod of the cotton plant.* Cotton is a cool, strong fiber, easy to wash, absorbent and therefore extremely pleasant to wear. Great advances have recently been made with easy-care finishes.	All cottons will be washable under Codes 1, 2 or 4, depending on their finish and color fastness.
Linen	*Linen is spun from the fibrous stalks of the flax plant.* Linen fabric is very tough, absorbent and cool to wear. Its strength actually increases in washing—thus its age-old use for sheets and household linen. Pure linen does crease, but new blends with man-made fibers and the development of crease-resistant finishes are making linen much more of an all-purpose fiber.	If washing is advised, Codes 1, 2 or 5 will apply. It is important to pay special attention to the instructions, because the treatment or finish given to linen fabrics may vary considerably.
Wool and animal fibers	*Wool fiber comes from the fleece of the sheep. Other animal fibers include the luxurious, and expensive, alpaca (alpaca goat or S. American llama); cashmere (very soft goat); vicuna (vicuna llama from S. America); mohair (crisp shiny fiber from the angora goat, used for men's lightweight suitings); and angora (angora rabbit).* Wool has inherent warmth and resilience. The most versatile of fibers, it can be spun and woven into both the lightest crepes or heaviest tweeds and is cool in summer, warm in winter.	Dry cleaning is recommended unless the article is stated as washable.
Silk	*Silk comes from the filament spun by the silkworm for its cocoon.* The most luxurious of fibers, silk has a lustrous, live quality and takes color to a deeper intensity than any other fiber.	Silk should be dry-cleaned unless stated as washable, when Code 7 is advised (warm water, do not rub, spin dry, do not wring)

What are man-made fibers?

Fiber family name	qualities	ways to wash
And Trade Names		
Acetate Acele, Celaperm, Chromspun, Estron	*Acetate is derived from cellulose, the raw materials of which are cotton linters or wood pulp.* Regarded as the most silk-like of the manmade fibers in wide use. Acetate drapes well, and is woven into satins, taffetas, brocades and surahs. It is extensively used for silk-like jersey, and linings.	100% acetate fabrics can be washed easily, in *warm* (not hot) water at Code 6. They should be washed frequently to avoid over-soiling, then ironed with a warm iron while still damp.
Acrylic Acrilan, Courtelle, Creslan, Orlon, Zefran	*Acrylic fibers are produced from acrylonitrile, a liquid derived from oil refining and coal carbonization processes.* Easy-care and crease-resistant, acrylic fibers most closely resemble wool and are very popular for knitwear and light, washable tweeds.	Acrylic fibers wash easily, under Codes 6 or 8, and dry quickly. A cold rinse should always be given before drying, to avoid creasing. Always iron *dry*—do not dampen for ironing.
Modacrylic Dynel, Verel	*Based on derivatives of oil refining and coal carbonization processes.* Modacrylic fibers are used for both garment and industrial fabrics. Strong, hard-wearing and flame-proof, they are very practical for children's clothing.	Washing at Code 6 is a simple matter, but only a cool iron should be used when the article is quite dry.
Elastomeric Glospun, Lycra, Numa, Vyrene	*These are stretch yarns with a high degree of elasticity, based on segmented polyurethane.* Elastomeric fibers are used in foundation garments, swimwear and stockings.	These fibers are always combined with others which dictate the washing intructions. Do not iron.
Nylon Antron, Blue C Nylon, Caprolan, Chemstrand Nylon, Dupont Nylon, Enkalon, Qiana	*Nylon's raw materials are benzene from coal, oxygen and nitrogen from the air and hydrogen from water.* Nylon is extremely strong and has inherent elasticity. It can be spun into fine silk-like fibers which make it ideal for stockings and lingerie. Its crease-resistance and quick-drying qualities have given nylon a large share of the men's shirt market.	Knitted as well as woven nylon fabrics shed creases and are easy to wash and quick to dry. White nylon should be laundered according to Code 3. Colored nylon at Code 4. It is often drip-dry and minimum or non-iron.
Polyester Avlin, Dacron, Encron, Fortrel, Kodel, Terylene, Trevira, Vycron	*Polyesters are made from ethylene glycol and terephthalic acid, derived from petroleum.* A very strong fiber, polyester is frequently found as a blend with wool or cotton. Used alone, polyester is often 'bulked' or 'crimped', and knitted to give a durable and practical fabric.	Woven or knitted into jersey fabrics, polyesters should be washed at Code 4, usually drip-dried and ironed only with a warm iron when necessary.
Triacetate Arnel	*Primary raw materials in the manufacture of triacetates are wood pulp and cotton linters.* Triacetates have a dry, crisp silky handle and slightly shiny finish. They have easy-care qualities and are crease-resistant.	Always washable, at Code 6 or Code 8 for permanently-pleated fabrics, triacetates are quick drying and require little or no ironing. Must not be dry-cleaned with trichlorethylene.
Viscose Rayon Avril, Bemberg, Coloray, Colorspun, Cupioni, Enka Rayon, Fortisan, Spunlo, Zantrel	*With a wood pulp base, viscose rayon is a cellulosic fiber and is probably the most widely used of all man-made fibers.* Rayon is the old 'art silk' rayon and is still used today for linings or 'brushed' as a cheap wool substitute. It is also used as a blend where its absorbency is balanced with a stronger but non-porous fiber.	100% viscose rayon fabrics may be washed at Codes 2, 4, 5 or 7, depending on the particular fiber content of the fabric, and individual instructions must be followed carefully. A medium-hot iron is usually suggested.

Processes and finishes

Crease resistance. Almost all fabrics have a tendency to crease and some, like pure linen, crease far more than others. To counteract this, the yarn or fabric is chemically treated to give it added springiness and resilience. Most crease-resist finishes radically alter the structure of the fiber throughout its life. Drip-dry and easy-care usually applies to garments like shirts and underwear and indicates that they should shed their creases if they are hung out to dry after washing. The question of whether or not to iron applies equally to non-iron, wash n' wear, as well as drip-dry and easy-care. Although you won't have to give your clothes the thorough going over a madras cotton shirt requires, they will look crisper and smarter if you do iron them lightly.
Trade marks: *Tebilized® Wrinkl-shed® Vitalized®*

Machine washability. What is so wonderful about machine washability, you may ask yourself as you sort through your load of dirty laundry. Practically everything—when you consider that the fabric in question is pure wool tweed and pure wool jersey and knitwear. The men behind the Woolmark guarantee have devised a process of treating wool yarn which prevents shrinkage. What to look for when buying clothes is Machine Washable or Washable, Shrink-Resistant on the label, followed by detailed washing instructions.

Pre-shrunk. Fabrics can stretch quite badly in manufacture. To correct this, and to prevent them from shrinking when washed at home, they are pre-shrunk as part of the finishing process. The pre-shrunk process often combines the same qualities as drip-dry and crease-resistant finishes.
Trade marks: *Sanforized® Tebilized®*

London shrunk. A famous finishing process applied to wool suitings which are moistened and then allowed to dry out naturally. This leaves them in the ideal condition for tailoring.
Trade marks: *Lanaset® Resloom®*

Permanent press. To pleat wool permanently, the fabric is chemically 'processed' and then fixed by steam pressing. More rigorous treatment can be given to man-made fibers and special blends. They are soaked with chemicals and then 'cured' by literally baking them at high temperatures in ovens! This process permanently sets pleats and creases and is particularly suitable for skirts and men's pants. The heat treatment is now being applied to entire garments which claim never to
300

crease, wrinkle, stretch or lose their shape and are also fully machine washable. At the moment this heat treatment mostly applies to men's wear, especially pants.

Fashioned. Fully fashioned denotes that knitwear or stockings have been 'fashioned' into shape on the knitting machine. Semi-fashioned applies to knitted garments that are only partially fashioned.

Mothproofing. There are distinct differences between mothproof and mothproofed. The first denotes fabrics which are inherently mothproof: For example no moth has the right kind of digestion to cope with acrylics or polyesters. The second applies to wool fabrics, something moths are especially fond of, and indicates that a garment is treated against moths for life. If you suspect repeated washing or drycleaning has removed the proofing, you can always take the proper precautions to discourage moths.
Trade marks: *Boconize® Erustomoth®*

Flameproofing. By law, many items have to be treated for flame resistance. However, this can wash out if you use soap or a detergent containing soap. One of the best answers is to make those items which should be flameproof from special fabrics, or have the finished garment flameproofed. Always wash flameproofed fabrics according to the directions.
Trade marks: *Banflame® Fire Chief® Flamefoil® Pyroset®*

Rainproofing. When does a shower become a downpour? When you discover your raincoat is only water-repellent, and not, as you might have hoped when you bought it, waterproof, and you get very wet. The words "Water-repellent", "Rain resist" or "Showerproof" sewed onto a tab inside your raincoat can mean it has been treated with silicones to resist a certain amount of water. Waterproof means one hundred percent resistance to rain and that the article is made from a rubberized or plastic-covered fabric or treated with wax. N.B. This term can only be applied to garments which have reinforced seams!
Chemicals: *Scotchgard® Zepel®*
Trade marks: *Aridex® Cravenette® Impregnole® Neva-Wet® Rainfoe®*

Luster finishes. A few years ago, when crisp cotton with a shiny finish was in fashion, resins and starches were applied to it to give a luster. This gloss finish is now primarily applied to home furnishing fabrics in the form of glazed chintz.
Trade marks: *Everglaze® Vita Glaze®*

Special note

The trade names, processes and finishes mentioned in this Take Care chapter are by no means a complete summary of those which are available. Creative Hands has merely selected for each category samples of what can be obtained easily on the American market today.

Useful definitions of fabric and fiber terms

Bulking or high bulk. A process which fluffs out the fibers of the yarn to give extra softness, stretch and absorbency. It also gives a pleasant, deeper texture particularly in knitted fabrics made from acrylics or polyesters.

Count. The yarn count indicates the thickness or fineness of cotton, wool or linen yarns. The higher the count the finer the yarn.

Denier. The same as count, but is used for silk and man-made filament yarns. As in stockings, the lower the denier figure the finer the yarn.

Mercerized. Cotton yarns, specially treated under tension, to make them extra strong, colorful and lustrous.

Spun yarns. Made from fibers spun to various thicknesses—from the softly spun yarns used for nice Shetland sweaters (woolen spun) to the fine, tight, smooth yarn (worsted spun) used for fine worsted suitings.

Warp. The lengthwise threads in woven fabrics.

Weft. The crosswise threads in woven fabrics.

Pattern Library

Appliqué flower

Motifs like this, cut from printed fabrics and appliquéd, give a quick effective decoration. This gay flower has been cut from a coarse linen drapery fabric and applied to a rich blue linen with zigzag machine stitching. It can just as easily be done by hand using buttonhole stitch. Embroider the veining on the flowers and leaves if you want to add more interest to the design.

There are many ways to apply the idea, such as using the leftover scraps from curtainmaking to appliqué onto a pillow or bedspread for a clever and detailed color scheme.

Double crossed stitches

You have already seen how you can alter the appearance of knitted stitches by working into the back of the stitch to produce a twisted effect. (Check back to the twisted stockinette stitch pattern in Knitting Know-how chapter 5, page 82.)

To give an even more pronounced twisted appearance, you use the method of actually crossing two or more stitches. This means that the second stitch on the left-hand needle is worked before the first so that the stitches change place, producing an attractive miniature cable or twisted rib effect.

There are countless variations of cable patterns, three of which are described in this chapter, together with their standard abbreviations.

Knitted crossed stitch with back twist (Tw2B)

The twist lies to the left. Pass the right-hand needle behind the first stitch on the left-hand needle, knit into the back of the next stitch and leave on the needle. Then knit into the back of the first stitch and slip both stitches off the left-hand needle onto the right-hand needle. (This is used in twisted rib pattern and mock cable.)

Knitted crossed stitch with front twist (Tw2F)

The twist lies to the right. Pass the right-hand needle in front of the first stitch on the left-hand needle and knit the next stitch, leaving it on the needle. Then knit the first stitch and slip both stitches off the left-hand needle onto the right-hand needle.

Purled crossed stitch with front twist (Tw2PF)

This is often used on a purl row when the purled side is the wrong side. It produces a crossed thread lying to the right on the knit side of the work. Pass the right-hand needle in front of the first stitch on the left-hand needle and purl the next stitch, leaving it on the needle. Then purl the first stitch and slip both stitches off the left-hand needle onto the right-hand needle.

Purled crossed stitch with back twist (Tw2PB)

Because this is more difficult to work, it is less often used. It forms a cross lying to the left on the knit side of the work. Pass the right-hand needle behind the first stitch on the left-hand needle, purl the next stitch through the back of the loop and leave it on the needle. Then purl the first stitch and slip both stitches off the left-hand needle onto the right-hand needle.

Sometimes it is easier to use a cable needle to help with this stitch. Slip the first stitch from the left-hand needle onto the cable needle and hold at the front of the work, purl the next stitch through the back of the loop and purl the stitch from the cable needle.

A slightly different, or mock, twist can be given to the stitches if each stitch is lifted over the first one before the first one is worked. This is not usually referred to by any standard abbreviation, but will be described in detail in the directions for knitting garments in which the stitch appears.

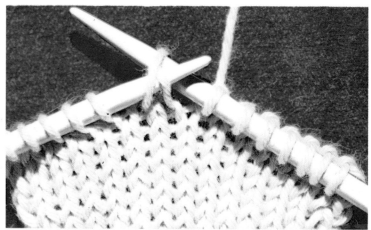

Knitted crossed stitch with back twist (Tw2B)

Purled crossed stitch with front twist (Tw2PF)

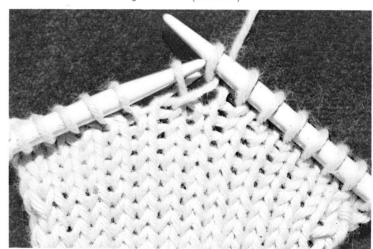

Crossing two stitches to the right (Cross 2R)

Crossing two stitches to the right (Cross 2R)

Pass the right-hand needle in back of the first stitch on the left-hand needle and knit into back loop of second stitch. Lift it over the first stitch and off the needle point. Knit the first stitch on the left-hand needle. (This is used in crossed miniature cable.)

Crossing two stitches to the left (Cross 2L)

Slip the first stitch on the left-hand needle without knitting it. Knit the next stitch on the left-hand needle and slip it onto the right-hand needle. Using the left-hand needle point, pass the slipped stitch over the newly knitted stitch, knitting into the slipped stitch at the same time.

Twisted rib pattern

Work over a number of stitches divisible by 14, plus 2.

1st row. P2, *Tw2B, P2, K4 all tbl, P2, Tw2B, P2, rep from * to end.

2nd row. K2, *P2, K2, P4, K2, P2, K2, rep from * to end.

Rep 1st and 2nd rows once.

5th row. P2, *Tw2B, P2, into 4th and 3rd sts on left-hand needle work Tw2B leaving sts on left-hand needle,

work Tw2B into 2nd and 1st sts on left-hand needle and slip all 4 sts from left- to right-hand needle,

P2, Tw2B, P2, rep from * to end.

6th row. As 2nd.

These 6 rows form the pattern and are repeated throughout.

Mock cable

Worked over a number of stitches divisible by 5, plus 3.

1st row. P3, *K2, P3, rep from * to end.

2nd row. K3, *P2, K3, rep from * to end.

Rep 1st and 2nd rows once.

5th row. P3, *Tw2B, P3, rep from * to end.

6th row. As 2nd.

These 6 rows form the pattern and are repeated throughout.

Crossed miniature cable

Worked over a number of stitches divisible by 7, plus 3.

1st row. P3, *K4, P3, rep from * to end.

2nd row. K3, *P4, K3, rep from * to end.

3rd row. P3, *(cross 2R) twice, P3, rep from * to end.

4th row. As 2nd.

These 4 rows form the pattern and are repeated throughout.

Right: twisted rib pattern
Below left: mock cable
Below right: crossed miniature cable

The prettiest suit in town (part 2)

With these instructions for crocheting a skirt to team with the jacket featured in the last Basic Wardrobe chapter, you now have all the ingredients for making yourself a delightful suit. There are also directions for a blouse to complete the outfit or to wear on its own as a separate top. A crocheted suit is perfect for town and country wear and is an indispensible item in every woman's wardrobe.

Sizes
Skirt: directions are for 34in hips.
Length, 18[20:22]in, adjustable.
Blouse: directions are for 32in bust.
The figures in brackets [] refer to the 36 and 38in hip sizes and 34 and 36in bust sizes.

Gauge
Skirt: 6½sts and 4¾ rows to 1in over patt using No.C crochet hook.
Blouse: 7sts and 5¼ rows to 1in over patt using No.C crochet hook.

Materials
Reynolds Parfait
30 gram balls
Skirt: 17[18:20] balls in main color, A
1 ball in contrast, B
Waist length grosgrain ribbon
7in skirt zipper
Blouse: 13[15:17] balls in contrast, B
Four small buttons
One No. C (2.50 mm) crochet hook
One No. B (2.00 mm) crochet hook

Skirt
(Back and front alike)

Using No.B crochet hook and A, ch133[141:149] and work 4 rows patt as given for jacket back (see the Basic Wardrobe chapter in Part 15). 132[140:148] sts. Change to No.C crochet hook and continue in patt until skirt measures 3[3¼:4]in from beg, ending with a 2nd patt row. If length requires altering, make an adjustment at this point. For example, if you want to make a longer skirt, you must add the extra length here before you begin the shaping.
Dec row 2sc in first 3 ch sp, 1sc in each of next 2 ch sp, patt to last 5 ch sp, 1sc in each of next 2 ch sp, 2sc in each of last 3 ch sp. 128 [136:144] sts.
Work without shaping until skirt measures 5½[7:8½]in from beg, ending with a 2nd patt row.
Work dec row. 124[132:140] sts. Work without shaping until 7½[9½:11½]in from beg.

Work dec row. 120[128:136] sts. Work without shaping until 9[11:13]in from beg.
Work dec row. 116[124:132] sts. Work without shaping until 10[12:14]in from beg.
Work dec row. 112[120:128] sts. Work 3 rows without shaping.
Dec 4sts as before on next and every following 4th row until 88[96:104] sts rem.
Work without shaping until 17[19:21]in from beg.
Change to No.B crochet hook. Work 1in sc.
Fasten off.

Finishing

Block and press each piece on WS, using a warm iron and damp cloth.
Using a flat seam, join side seams, leaving 7in free on left side for zipper.
Sew zipper in place.
Sew grosgrain inside waist.
Press seams.

Blouse back

Using No.B crochet hook, ch115[121:130].
1st row 1sc in 2nd ch from hook, 1sc in each ch to end. Turn. 114[120:129] sts.
2nd row Ch2, 1sc in each st to end.
Turn.
Change to No.C crochet hook.
1st row (right side) Ch3 to form first dc, skip first st, *skip next st, ch1, 1dc in each of next 2sts, rep from * to last 2sts, skip next st, ch1, 1dc in last st. Turn.
2nd row 1sc in first st, *1ss in next ch, ch2, 1ss in same ch, ch2, skip 2sts, rep from * ending with 1ss in last ch, ch2, 1ss in same ch, 1sc in 3rd of ch3. Turn.
3rd row Ch3 to form first dc, *ch1, 2dc in 2 ch sp, rep from * ending with ch1, 1dc in last st. Turn.
The 2nd and 3rd rows form the patt and are rep throughout.
Work in patt without shaping until back measures 14in from beg, ending with a 3rd patt row.

Shape armholes
1st row Ss across 6sts, patt to last 6sts. Turn.
2nd row Patt.
3rd row Ss across 3sts, patt to last 3sts. Turn.
Rep 2nd and 3rd rows 3[4:5] times more. 78[78:81] sts. **
Work without shaping until back measures 17½in, ending with a 2nd patt row.

Divide for back opening
32in and 34in sizes only
Next row Ch3, (ch1, 2dc in next 2 ch sp) 12 times, ch1, 1dc in next 2 ch sp. Turn. 39sts.
36in size only
Next row Ch3, (ch1, 2dc in next 2 ch sp) 13 times. Turn.
Work without shaping on these sts until back measures 21[21½:21½]in, ending at neck edge.

Shape shoulder
1st row Patt to last 12sts. Turn.
2nd row Patt.
3rd row Patt to last 9sts. Fasten off.
32in and 34in sizes only
Attach yarn to center 2 ch sp, ch3, patt to end. Work to correspond to other side.
36in size only
Skip center st, attach yarn to next 2 ch sp, patt to end. Work to correspond to other side.

Front

Work as for back to **
Work without shaping until front measures 18½[19:19]in, ending with a 2nd patt row.

Shape neck
1st row Patt across 30sts. Turn.
2nd row Patt.
3rd row Patt to last 3sts. Turn.
Rep 2nd and 3rd rows twice more. 21sts.
Work without shaping until front measures same as back to shoulder, ending at armhole.

Shape shoulder
1st row Ss across 12sts, patt to end.
2nd row As patt row 9.
Fasten off.

Skip center 18[18:21] sts,
attach yarn, patt to end.
Next row Patt.
Next row Ss across 3sts,
patt to end. Work to
correspond to other side.

Neck edging

Sew shoulder seams.
With RS facing and No.B
crochet hook, work 3 rows sc
around neck over an odd
number of sts.

Work picot edge
Next row 1ss in first st,
*1ss in next st, ch3, 1ss
in same st, 1ss in next st,
rep from * to end.
Fasten off.

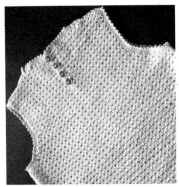

Picot edging on blouse back

Armhole edgings
Work as for neck edging.

Finishing

Block and press on WS, using
a warm iron and damp cloth.
Using a flat seam, join side
seams.
With WS facing and No.B
crochet hook, work picot edge
around lower edge, working
into the ch loop only.
With RS facing, work 1 row
sc along RS of back opening.
Next row Work in sc, making
4 button loops evenly spaced.
Button loops are made by
skipping 3sts and working
ch3.
Next row Work in sc
working 3sc into each ch3
button loop.
Work 2 rows sc along left
side. Overlap right over left
and secure at bottom. Sew on
buttons. Press seams.

Three-piece suit in crochet ▶

Crochet yourself a cross

Crochet
Know-how

16

It is simple to make crisp and easily laundered place mats or tray cloths with these cross patterns and an edging, or you can work more motifs to give any size and shape you want. Once you see how stunning the mats are, you can progress to working an impressive dinner cloth or a bedspread — perhaps in white backed with plain fabric in a subtle color to show up the design.

George Cross mat
Materials
9 balls of Coats & Clark's O.N.T. Speed Cro-Sheen. 100 yd. balls
One No. B (2.00 mm) crochet hook.
Each square measures about 2¼in and the completed mat, made from 48 squares, measures 22in by 17½in. The number of squares you use can be altered to make mats in all sorts of different sizes and shapes.
Ch12. Join to form a circle with a ss into first ch.
1st round Ch2, work 23sc into circle. Join with a ss into 2nd of first 2ch.
2nd round Ch4, 1tr into each of next 2sc, *ch7, 1tr into each of next 6sc, rep from * twice, ch7, 1tr into each of next 3sc. Join with a ss into 4th of first 4ch.
3rd round Ch2, 1sc between each of next 2tr, *4sc into ch7 sp, ch2, 4sc into same ch sp, 1sc between each of next 6tr, rep from * twice, 4sc into ch7 sp, ch2, 4sc into ch7 sp, 1sc between each of next 2tr. Join with a ss into 2nd of first 2ch. Break yarn

and fasten off.
Work 47 more squares.
If desired sew two crossed stitches in center as shown.
Join squares
Place 2 squares together, RS facing. Attach yarn into corner ch of both squares with a ss. Work through both edges, working 1sc in each stitch to end of side.
Join other squares in same way. The mat has 8 squares in one row and a total of 6 rows.
Edging
Join with a ss to left-hand corner of any square on the outside.
1st round Ch6, *1sc into each of next 7sc, ch4, rep from * to last 6sc, 1sc into each of next 6sc. Join with a ss into 2nd of first 6ch. The picot formed by the ch4 should come at the corners and center of each square. Where squares are joined together, the corner picot comes in line with the seam.
2nd round Ch2, 1sc into center of picot, ch8, *2sc into next picot, ch8, rep from * to end of round. Join with a ss into 2nd of first 2ch.
3rd round *Into each ch8 sp work 5sc, ch2, 5sc, rep from * to end of round. Join with a ss into first sc.
4th round Work 1ss into each sc to first picot of previous round, ch2, 1sc into same picot, ch8, *2sc into next picot, ch8, rep from * to last picot before corner, 2sc into last picot, ch8, 2sc into corner 8ch, 2sc into first picot of next side 8ch.
Continue to work other sides and corners in the same

way. Join with a ss into 2nd of first 2ch.
5th round As 3rd.
6th round Work 1ss into each sc to first picot, 1sc in same picot, ch8, *2sc into next picot, ch8, rep from * to end of round. Join with a ss into 2nd of first 2ch.
7th round Ch2, *11sc into next ch8 sp, 1sc between sc at end of ch sp, rep from * to end of round. Join with a ss into 2nd of first 2ch. Break yarn and fasten off. Pin out mat and press under a damp cloth with a warm iron.

Victoria Cross mat
Materials
6 balls of Coats & Clark's O.N.T. Speed Cro-Sheen. 100 yd. balls
One No. B (2.00 mm) crochet hook.
Each square measures about 3¾ in. and the completed mat, made from 18 squares, measures 27 in. by 15¾ in.
Ch12. Join to form a circle with a ss into first ch.
1st round Ch2, work 23sc into circle. Join with a ss into 2nd of first 2ch.
2nd round Ch5, (1tr, ch1) into each of next 3sc, ch6, *skip 2sc, (1tr, ch1) into each of next 4sc, ch6, rep from * twice. Join with a ss into 4th of first 5ch.
3rd round Ch2, 1sc between first 2tr, work 1sc, ch4, 1sc all between next 2tr, 2sc between next 2tr, into ch6 sp work 4sc, ch4, 4sc, *2sc into first sp between tr of next group, 1sc, ch4, 1sc all into 2nd sp, 2sc into 3rd sp, 4sc, ch4, 4sc all into ch6 sp, rep from * twice. Join with a ss into 2nd of first 2ch.
4th round Ch5, 1tr into first sc, ch4, skip ch4 forming picot and 2sc on each side of picot, *(1tr, ch1) into each of next 4sc, ch5, skip next picot and 1sc on each side of picot, (1tr, ch1) into next 4sc, ch3, skip picot and 2sc on each side of picot, rep from * twice, (1tr, ch1) into each of next 4sc, ch5, skip picot and 1sc on side of picot, (1tr, ch1) into each of next 2sc. Join with a ss into 4th

of first 5ch.
5th round Ch2, 1sc between next 2tr, *4sc into ch4 sp, 2sc between each tr of 4tr group, into ch6 sp work 3sc, picot of ch2, 3sc, work 2sc between each tr of next group, rep from * twice, 4sc into ch4 sp, 2sc between each tr of group, into ch6 sp work 3sc, ch2, 3sc, 2sc between each of next 2tr. Join with a ss into 2nd of first 2ch. Break yarn and fasten off. Work 17 more squares. Join squares as for George Cross mat, making 3 rows of 6 squares.

Edging
Join yarn with a ss into center of side at right-hand corner of square.
1st round Ch2, *1sc into each sc, rep from * to corner 2ch, ch2. Work other sides and corners in same way. Join with a ss into 2nd of first 2ch.
2nd round Ch5, (1tr, ch1) into each of next 2sc, ch3, *skip 6sc, (1tr, ch1) into next 6sts, ch3, rep from * to 3sc before corner 2ch, (1tr, ch1) into each of next 3sc, into corner 2ch work 4tr, ch1, (1tr, ch1) into next 3sc, ch3, **(1tr, ch1) into each of next 6sc, skip 6sc, ch3, rep from ** to next corner.
Work other sides and corners in same way. Join with a ss into 4th of first 5ch.
3rd round Ch2, 1sc into next sp between 4th and 5th tr of group, 1sc into next sp, *4sc into ch4 sp, 1sc into first sp of group, 2sc into 2nd sp, 1sc, ch4, 1sc all into 3rd sp, 2sc into 4th sp, 1sc into 5th sp, rep from * to corner group, work 1sc into each of next 4 sp, then 1sc, ch4, 1sc all into corner sp, 1sc into each of next 4 sp. Work other sides and corners in this way. Join with a ss into 2nd of first 2ch.
4th round Ss to last st of 6tr group, ch5, (1tr, ch1) into next 5sc, ch3, * (1tr, ch1) into 6sc above next ch sp, ch3, rep from *

306

The George Cross motif
Place mats in contrasting colors ▶

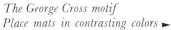

to corner group, into corner
ch4 work 3tr, ch4, 3tr.
Work other sides and corners
in same way. Join with a ss
into 4th of first 5ch.
5th round Ch2, 2sc into 2nd
sp of 6tr group, into 3rd sp
work 1sc, ch4, 1sc, into 4th
sp work 2sc, into 5th sp 1sc,
*into ch4 sp work 2sc, ch4,
2sc, into first sp of 6tr
group work 1sc, into 2nd sp
work 2sc, into 3rd sp work
1sc, ch4, 1sc, into 4th sp
work 2sc, into 5th sp work
1sc, rep from * to corner,
work 1sc into each sp
between 3tr, into ch4 work
2sc, ch4, 2sc, work 1sc into
each sp of 3tr group.
Complete other sides and
corners in this way. Join with
a ss into 2nd of first 2ch.
6th round Ss to first picot of
ch4, *1sc into picot, ch6,
rep from * to end. Join with
a ss into first sc.
7th round Ch2, into next ch6
sp work 3sc, ch4, 4sc, *into
next ch6 sp work 4sc, ch4,
4sc, rep from * to end. Join
with a ss into 2nd of first 2ch.
Break yarn, fasten off and
complete as for George
Cross mat.

The Victoria Cross motif

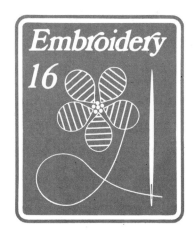

The art of appliqué

Appliqué is simply the technique of applying one fabric to another. It originated as an imaginative way of patching worn clothes, but it has become a highly developed form of decoration—its present-day popularity is probably due to the fact that it is quick to do and that it makes use of all sorts of fabric scraps. This chapter provides the essential tips on choice of fabrics and the methods of appliqué. Embroidery chapter 17, page 328, suggests ways to create your own designs, and gives step-by-step instructions for basic appliqué.

Basic hints

Choosing materials

The applied materials should be of equal or lighter weight than the background material, but the background material can be mounted on strong cotton to add strength if desired. Non-fraying fabrics are the easiest to apply, as the edges don't have to be

Start with bold appliqué on nursery pillows or children's aprons

turned in. If you want to use an attractive material which might fray, iron on a woven adhesive interfacing to the wrong side of the fabric to prevent this.

Applying materials

If the appliqué is going to receive hard wear, remember to match the grain of the two fabrics to prevent puckering and splitting. Fabrics such as felt do not have a grain, so these can be applied in any position.

To work in the hand or in a frame

For appliqué it is best to work with the background material pulled taut, in a rectangular frame, an old picture frame or, for small items, an embroidery hoop on a stand. Very small pieces may be worked in the hand if you wish, but whether you use a frame or not, be sure to stretch the fabric to be applied as much as the background material. If the fabrics are at different tensions it will eventually cause puckering and spoil the look of your work.

Using a rectangular frame

One type of frame is made up of four strips of wood—two strong cross bars joined by two side bars with peg holes to vary the size. Another type of rectangular frame works on the same principle, but differs from it in that the side bars are threaded for screwing the fabric taut.

The frame with peg holes is preferable to the other rectangular frame for anything but very lightweight fabrics, because the screw rings on the frame can work loose and relax the tension of the fabric while you stitch.

There are two kinds of rectangular frames on the market—hand frames and floor-standing frames. Hand frames adjust to 28in wide and floor frames to 40in wide. Whether you use a frame with a stand or not is up to you, but generally it is easier to work with a stand.

Mounting fabric on a frame

1. Mark the center of the webbing on the frame rollers with a basting line.
2. On the top and bottom of the fabric, make a $\frac{1}{2}$in turning to the wrong side, and hem it if it is likely to fray.
3. Mark the centers of these turned edges with pins. Place the center of the fabric to the center of the webbing and pin from the center outward.
4. Using very strong thread, whip the 2 edges together, always working from the center outward.
5. Repeat on second roller.
6. Adjust the side bars until the fabric is taut.
7. Baste 1in tape to the sides of the fabric, using small stitches.
8. Thread a large needle with strong string, and lace through the webbing and over the slats with stitches about 1in apart.
9. Leave about 18in of string at each end. Pull the string taut and wind it around the ends of the frame, then tie to secure.

Framing a fabric with backing

It is best to use a backing such as white (or unbleached) strong cotton such as muslin. Make sure backing is pre-shrunk and at least one inch bigger all around than the fabric to be embroidered.
1. Baste a line down the center of the backing and of the fabric to be embroidered.
2. Place the fabric on the backing, matching the center lines. Pin it into place, working out from the center with the pins pointing inward to avoid puckering. Do not stretch either layer.
3. Firmly baste around the outside edge through both fabrics. Remove the pins.
4. Now mount the backed fabric in the frame according to the previous instructions.

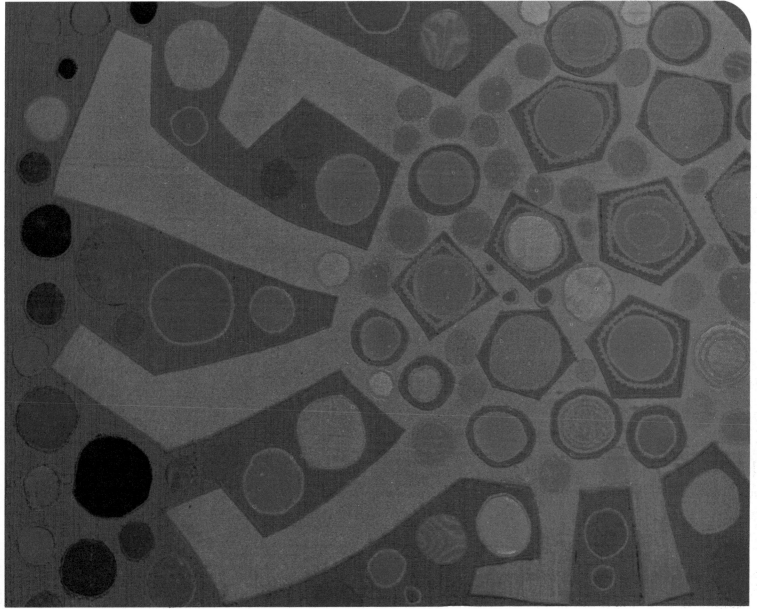

Part of a modern design, called Mexican Sun, which shows the stunning results of combining appliqué and simple embroidery stitches, using the cut and stitch method. Zigzag machine stitching has been used to join the pieces to the background and couching and double knot stitch as surface decoration.

Which method do I choose?

There are several appliqué methods—which one you choose depends on the type of material you want to use or the effect you wish to achieve. Here are the main methods.

Stick and stitch
This is the simplest form of appliqué. Simply stick cut-outs of non-fraying materials with a fabric glue onto a fabric background and secure the edges with either hand or machine stitches.

Cut and stitch
This method is best for firm non-fraying materials which you can safely cut to shape and slip stitch by hand, or zigzag stitch on a swing-needle sewing machine over the raw edges. You can then decorate the applied areas with various kinds of stitching.

Stitch and cut
This method is used on thin fabrics which would fray if cut out before applying. Cut a larger area than you need, marking the exact shape required, then either buttonhole stitch by hand or zigzag by machine onto the main fabric. Then trim off the surplus appliqué fabric very close to the stitching, using a pair of really sharp scissors.

Blind appliqué
This is another method for materials which fray easily. Turn the edges under and baste into position (around a cardboard template if it is a difficult shape), before applying. Press the turnings flat and slip stitch the shape into position. A bulky fabric will be easier to apply if you cut across corners and clip into curves. This will make the shapes neater and help them lie flat.

Cut-outs
This is a reversed appliqué method. Baste two or more layers of fabric together and cut out the shapes to reveal the underneath layer or layers. Then either buttonhole stitch the raw edges or sew down a small turning with a slip stitch, or secure the shape with a straight or zigzag line of machine stitching. You can back the cut-outs with different colored fabrics or ribbons.

A bold
and beautiful
bolero

This beautiful bolero is specially designed for Creative Hands, with two color schemes to choose from. On this page is the graph for the pattern—turn over for the embroidery chart.

What you will need to make the bolero:
- ☐ ¾yd double-weave canvas with 10 double threads to 1in
- ☐ ¾yd corduroy or velvet 36in wide for back of bolero
- ☐ 1¼yd lining 36in wide
- ☐ 2yds folded braid
- ☐ Sewing thread
- ☐ D.M.C. Tapestry yarn
- ☐ Soft lead pencil
- ☐ Large sheet of paper

The pattern

Simply copy the pattern for your size from the graph on this page onto paper drawn with 1in squares. Cut out the pattern. The graph pattern is given in 34in and 36in bust sizes only, but you can use a commercial bolero pattern in a larger size if you need to. Simply extend background stitching over the extra canvas. For larger sizes remember to check yardage and background yarn amounts.

Transfer the outline for the bolero fronts onto the canvas by basting the pattern in place, then drawing around the edge and into the darts accurately with a soft pencil. Now work the design onto both sections (full design details on next page). Complete the needlepoint before cutting out the fronts, as you need the rectangle of canvas to enable you to set the work up in a frame. (It is essential to work a piece this size on a frame to keep it in shape.)

Working the design

The original design was worked in half cross-stitch with the centers of some of the flowers in slanting Gobelin stitch and cross-stitch. You can add more texture stitches if you wish, but be careful not to use too many or you may detract from the design itself. Or, if you prefer, you can use tent stitch throughout. Work the stitches right up to the traced edges and just over the dart line, so that no canvas shows when the darts are closed.

Cutting out

When the design is completed, block and trim the canvas as described in Needlepoint chapter 5, page 112, leaving ⅝in allowances on shoulder and side seams only. Trim the canvas as close to all other edges as possible without cutting into the stitching. Cut out the back of the bolero from the corduroy and then cut out lining to match both the back and the fronts, adding ⅝in seam allowances on the side and shoulder seams.

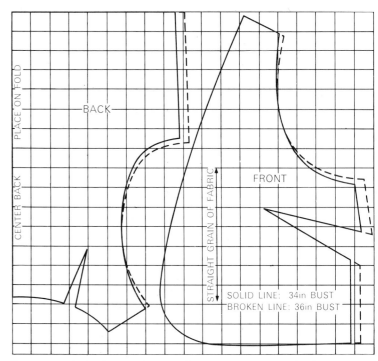

Pattern graph for front and back of bolero. Each sq = 1in. Solid line = 34in bust, broken line = 36in bust. Pattern is without seam allowance.

Within graph: PLACE ON FOLD · CENTER BACK · BACK · STRAIGHT GRAIN OF FABRIC · FRONT · SOLID LINE: 34in BUST · BROKEN LINE: 36in BUST

Making the bolero

Sew the darts on the bolero fronts either by machine or with a firm backstitch. Slash up the center of the dart and press it open with a slightly damp cloth and a medium hot iron. Trim away canvas to ⅝in, tapering off to point of dart. Stitch darts on back of bolero and stitch side and shoulder seams. Press seams open. Stitch the lining in the same way and then place bolero and lining together, wrong sides facing. Baste around edge of bolero and around armholes, matching up seams of lining to those of bolero. Work a line of machine stitching or backstitch ¼in in from all edges and then cover with braid as follows:

Turn under ⅝in at one end of the braid and start pinning it to the right side of the bolero from a side seam. Stretch the braid slightly as you pin so that it lies smoothly around the curves. Join the two ends of braid neatly. Sew the braid on the right side with a small, neat hem stitch and then hem braid to lining. Use thread the color of the braid.

▼ *One front worked in the alternative color combination* ► *The bolero*

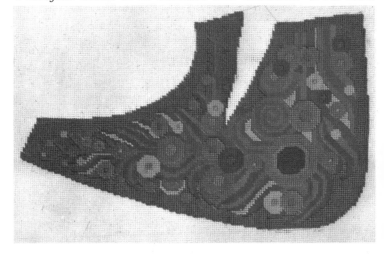

Simply work the design from this chart. Each square represents one half cross-stitch.

Normally it is usual to start working a charted design from the center, but in this case it is vitally important to commence working from the point of the dart. This will insure accurate placing of the design so that it will fit into the shaping of the bolero.

Yarn quantities

The numbers in the charts below refer to D.M.C. Tapestry Yarn colors.

Area		Blue/Green Color Combination Yarn Number	Red/Olive Color Combination Yarn Number	Skein Quantities
Background	□	lime 7504	olive 7485	7
Leaves	◼	blue 7797	red 7600	4
Leaves	◤	green 7909	orange 7946	4
Leaves	⊞	gray 7618	pink 7204	2
Flowers	⊙	blue 7996	blue 7241	3
Flowers and Flower Centers	⊡	mauve 7895	pink 7153	2
Flowers	⊙	pink 7132	orange 7947	2
Flowers	▼	purple 7243	magenta 7157	2
Large Flower Centers	▷	slate blue 7294	dark pink 7136	1
Flower Centers	⊠	blue 7316	mauve 7314	2
Flower Centers	⊠	green 7548	pale green 7351	2
Flower Centers	⊡	dusty pink 7124	salmon pink 7853	1

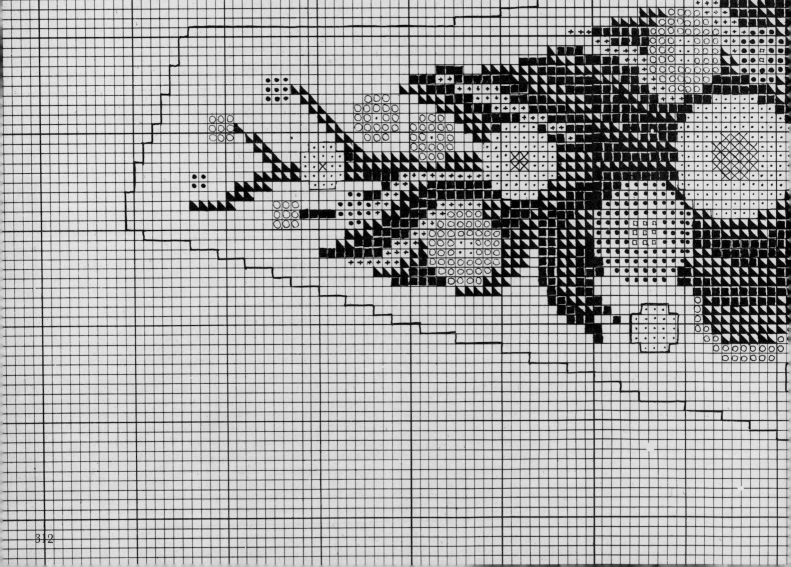

Introduction to basic netting

Netting is one of the oldest traditional crafts in the world, and yet despite its simplicity, hand-made netting is fast dying out. Here we show you the basis of this fascinating craft, and later you will be able to make your own nets for bed canopies, shopping bags and even square mesh net for embroidering.

Materials you will need

String. Ordinary cotton string is perfectly adequate, but once you have mastered the craft of netting you may want to experiment with colored strings and macramé-type cords.

Netting needle. These are the string holders, usually made of flexible and almost unbreakable plastic. They vary in width; most useful are medium (approximately $\frac{3}{4}$ inch wide), small ($\frac{1}{2}$ inch wide), and large ($\frac{7}{8}$ inch wide).

Mesh stick. The mesh stick performs two functions. It determines the size of the mesh and insures that the meshes are all equal in size. The mesh stick must always be wider than the needle so that the loaded needle will pass comfortably through the meshes. Mesh sticks can be improvised from rulers, but ideally they should be made from plastic 6 to 8 inches long and rectangular in shape.

Toggle. This is made from a button. Thread a fine string through two of the holes of the button and tie a reef knot below the button. It is used to suspend circular netting for bags so that it rotates freely during working.

314

Netting 1

Working base. A weighted cushion is used from which to work the netting. One very effective method is to cover an ordinary brick with several layers of flannel or fine wool, possibly pieces from an old skirt or a pair of pants. Or, more simply, netting can be suspended from a firmly secured hook.

The basic netting knot

Practice with two pieces of fairly thick string, each about 18 inches long. Tie one piece into a loop and attach it to your working base as a foundation loop. Using the second piece of string, pass all except the last two inches through from the back of the foundation loop and hold at the intersection with the thumb and one finger of the left hand. Holding the long end of the string (the working end) in the right hand, throw an open loop over to the left. Be careful not to allow a twist in this loop. With the right hand, take the end of the string to the right across the front of the foundation loop, around the back and out to the front through the thrown loop. Keeping the left thumb and finger firmly in position until the last moment, pull the knot firm. Make sure to seat the knot correctly around the bottom of foundation loop and do not let it slip below.

Loading the needle

Cut the length of string required. Hold the needle in the left hand with the point upward. Hold the end of the string anywhere on the body

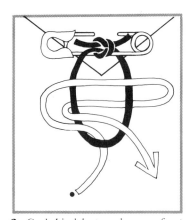

1. *Pass through loop from the back*

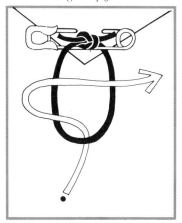

2. *Throw a loop across to the left*

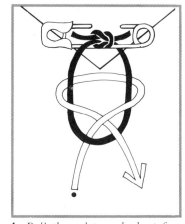

3. *Go behind loop and across front*

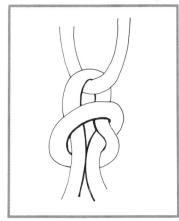

4. *Pull the end to make knot firm*

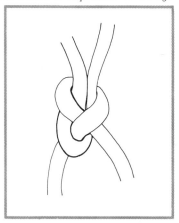

Correct seating of a netting knot

of the needle with the left thumb. Run the string up the body, around the prong and down the same side of the body to trap the starting end of the string. Take the string around the bottom or heel of the needle between the two projections. Turn the needle back to front, still with the point upward, and continue loading by repeating the same process.

To work a piece of netting

For this first practice piece, use a medium netting needle and a $1\frac{1}{2}$ inch-wide mesh stick. Make

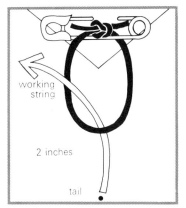

Wrong seating of a netting knot

a foundation loop with a piece of medium string 18 inches long. Load 6 yards of medium string onto the needle. Fasten the foundation loop to your working base and attach the string as before to the bottom of the foundation loop with a netting knot.

First row. Hold the mesh stick from below with the left hand, thumb at the front. Lay the working string over the front of the mesh stick, taking it around, below and up behind the stick and out through the

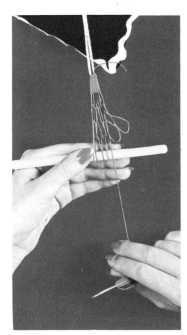

Working piece of diagonal netting

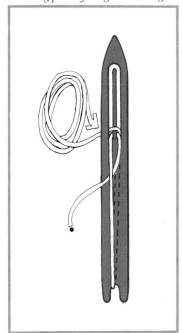

Loading the netting needle

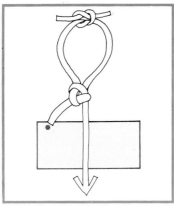

1. *Lay string over mesh stick front*

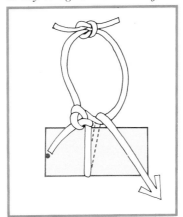

2. *Forming the first loop*

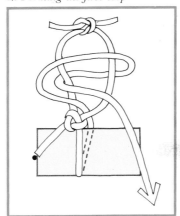

3. *Fixing mesh with a netting knot*

4. *Mesh stick with two loops*

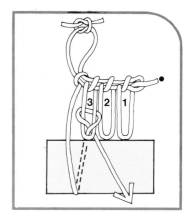

5. *Making first loop on second row*

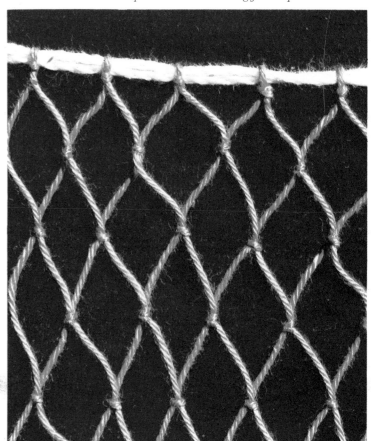

Close-up of a piece of diagonal netting

foundation loop from the back. Pull the needle downward with your right hand and the mesh stick will be hauled by pulley effect close up to the bottom of the foundation loop. With the left-hand thumb at the front and index finger at the back, hold the string and the foundation loop where they cross at the top of the mesh stick. Form the knot and draw it firm.

The mesh stick remains in position, encircled by this first loop and held in the left hand. The needle and working string

should automatically be over the front of the mesh stick and ready to continue by repeating the process. Obviously the mesh stick cannot move, but be sure to pull down with the right hand so that the knot is always made close to the top of the mesh stick. Unless you do so, your meshes will not be uniform and the net will be badly shaped.

Keeping the mesh stick in position with the left hand, repeat twice so that there are three loops on the mesh stick. Do not count the knots at the

top but the bottom of the loops formed on the mesh stick.

Second row. Remove the mesh stick. With the left hand turn the three newly made loops so that the last made loop is on the left ready to be used in the second row. As before form a loop around the mesh stick and knot the first loop. Be careful not to include the descending strand on the left as well as the two strands of the first loop. To avoid this, hold the intersection with the thumb and second finger of the left hand and use the left index

finger to mark the space between the descending strand and the first loop, the space in fact through which your needle will pass as it comes around the back of the loop.

This makes the first full mesh. Until now what have been called loops were in fact half meshes. Keep the mesh stick in position and mesh into the remaining two loops.

Third and subsequent rows. Remove the mesh stick only at the end of each row and continue meshing successive rows, always working left to right.

315

The basic blouse

This chapter introduces a new method for fitting—the muslin, a mock-up version of the final garment, also called a toile. This method is used by professional dressmakers to insure a perfect fit, and is well worth the extra effort involved.

The directions given here are for the green basic blouse with pointed cuffs and the floral, roll-up sleeved version. Directions for the other variations are given in later chapters.

Choosing the fabric

Choosing the fabric for making a blouse is exciting because there is such a variety of light-weight materials available—plain, patterned or textured. The most suitable fabrics for making the basic short-sleeved blouse and variation shown in the photograph opposite are those which are crisp enough to hold the tailored shape of this blouse. These are listed below. A list of fabrics which are more suitable for the other versions of the basic blouse, shown in the drawings opposite, will be included later, with the instructions for these styles.

Firmly woven cottons: poplin, men's shirting, Swiss cotton, lawn, piqué.

Linens: embroidered or other fine blouse-weight linen.

You should only use the fabrics listed below if you have a little practical experience in handling finer fabrics:

Silks, pure and artificial: shantung, Honan and fine Thai silk.

Man-made fibers: woven

Dacron or Acrilan or similar acrylic and polyester fibers; triacetate and rayon fabrics.

Materials

The yardage needed for the basic green blouse with pointed cuffs is given on the layout sheet in the Pattern Pack. For the floral, roll-up sleeved variation the yardages are the same except for the following sizes, which all need $\frac{1}{4}$yd extra: sizes $32\frac{1}{2}$ and 34, on 54in wide fabric, without one way; sizes 36 and 38, on 36in wide fabric without one way, and on 54in wide fabric with and without one way; sizes 40 and 42, on 36in wide fabric without one way, and on 54in wide fabric with and without one way.

When you are buying your fabric, remember that you will also need four buttons and matching thread.

Fitting with a muslin

The basic pattern is cut to standard measurements. But even if you are lucky enough to have perfect proportions, certain pattern adjustments may be necessary.

The correct way of finding this out before cutting the fabric is to make a muslin. This is a mock-up version of a garment, in this case a fitted bodice, which acts as a blueprint of your own measurements which can then be transferred to the paper pattern.

A muslin saves endless fitting problems later on, and you can use this same muslin when making up commercial paper patterns, to check where they need altering.

Making the bodice muslin

You will need the following materials:

☐ 1$\frac{1}{4}$yd 36in wide muslin or sheeting (which you can buy from dress fabric or large department stores)
☐ Paper for patterns
☐ A tailor's square or 45° set square
☐ Two pencils (one colored)
☐ Ruler

▼ The basic blouse pattern
This is used to make . . .

▼ . . . the muslin pattern
This is a waist-length version of the basic pattern, from which you cut . . .

▼ . . . the bodice muslin
This is a mock garment, in this case a fitted bodice.
The alterations on the muslin are used to make . . .

▼ . . . the new pattern
This is your personalized, adjusted and corrected pattern from which the blouse is cut.

Making the muslin pattern

Measure the length from your neck to your waistline, at back and front (see Dressmaking chapter 2, page 32), and mark off these measurements on the back and front pattern pieces. Lay the back and front pattern pieces together at the side seam with the lower stitching line of the side bust dart meeting the balance mark on the back section. Draw a pencil line across both pattern pieces to connect the waistline marks. This will give you the pattern length required for the muslin. Lay these pattern pieces on a large sheet of paper. Draw around the edges and into the darts. Mark the waistline and balance marks. Then copy the penciled waist onto the muslin pattern.

Cut out and trim the muslin pattern at the waist.

Cutting the bodice muslin

Fold the muslin or sheeting lengthwise. Place the back section of the muslin pattern on the fold line and the front section on the selvages.

Allow at least 1in seam allowance at all seam edges, except at the center front where it wraps over, and at least 2in at the waist.

Transfer all the pattern markings onto the fabric, then cut out and remove the pattern.

Open up the cut fabric pieces and draw in the grain lines of the fabric with colored pencil.

Marking the grain lines on the muslin

To find the lengthwise grain, measure about $3\frac{1}{2}$in away from the center back and the center front lines and draw a line parallel to each of these.

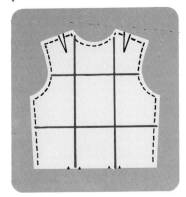

To find the crosswise grain on each piece, lay a tailor's square or 45° set square on the center back and center front and draw lines across the fabric halfway between the waistline and the side bust dart and halfway between shoulder and underarm seam.

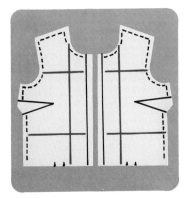

Fitting the muslin

Pin and baste the shoulder and side seams and darts. Do not baste the pleats in the waistline, as they will be pinned into darts when you fit the muslin. Try on the bodice over a full slip. Pin the fronts together down the center front line. Always start fitting from the shoulders downward, working toward the waist.

1

2

3

4

Other versions of the basic pattern: 1. Mandarin collar. 2. Shirt with top stitching and tails. 3. Sleeveless blouse. 4. Shirt version. Not shown: tie-neck blouse.

Two moods of the basic blouse—instructions for both are given here

Fitting the muslin...

Neck and armholes

1. Problem The muslin is too tight and pulls or is raised around the neck or at the armholes, or both.

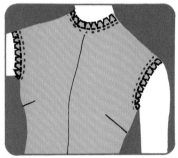

Correction If it's the neckline that is tight, snip into the seam allowance.
Mark a new neckline with a pencil on the muslin around the base of the neck and snip to this line until the garment sits smoothly without straining.
The correction is exactly the same for the armholes.

2. Problem Thin arms. The armhole is therefore too large.

Correction Raise the underarm curve into seam allowance.
318

3. Problem Thin neck. The neckline is therefore too large.

Correction Use the seam allowance on the muslin to mark the correct position for the neckline. If the neckline is still not the right size, you will have to baste strips of fabric around the neck on which to mark the new stitching line.

Shoulders

4. Problem Broad, straight shoulders.
The fabric strains at the outer end of the shoulder seam.

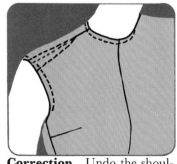

Correction Undo the shoulder seam and let it out.

5. Problem Very sloping shoulders.
The seam rises above the shoulder at the outer edge and there are often drag lines from the inner shoulder toward the underarm.

Correction Take the surplus material into the shoulder seam. Snip the seam allowance around the underarm curve, lifting the material on the front section until you have a smooth fit over the shoulders. Do the same for the back and watch the crosswise grain.

6. Problem Shoulders too wide or too narrow.

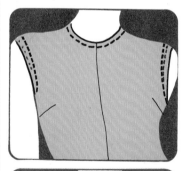

Correction To find the position for the armhole seam,

follow the crease of your underarm around the front onto the top of outer shoulder points. Continue working this line toward the back. When halfway down the back, move your arm forward very slightly and continue to work toward the crease of the underarm. This is to allow ease for movement.

Back

7. Problem Rounded back. This often accompanies round shoulders.
The horizontal grain lines tilt down toward the side seams.

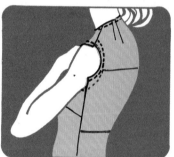

Correction Undo the side seams. Lift the back side seams until the grain is straight, and pin. Use the balance marks as a guide to see that you get the same lift on each side. Rip the shoulder seam, then lift the fullness around the armhole into the shoulder seam by deepening the dart.
If the problem is very pronounced, undo the shoulder darts and take the depth of the darts and the surplus fabric into the neckline by making two darts on each side of the center back.
Repin the shoulder seams and mark a new armhole line to match up with the line on the front section, because the original line will have moved in on the shoulder. Re-mark the

Color key to fitting the bodice muslin		Problem: color	▬
Original seamline	– – –	Correction: color	▬
New seamline	– – –	Grain lines	—
		Important	

underarm line, which has also been displaced, but allow plenty of width across the back.

8. Problem Straight, very erect back.
The horizontal grain lines drop at the back toward the center.

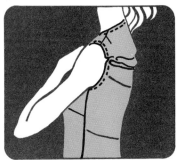

Correction If the drop is between the neck and underarm, pin a fold right across the back section, starting at the center, until the grain runs straight. Any fullness below that point can be let down into the waist seam, but only as far as the straight of the grain will allow. If this isn't enough, you will have to pin another fold line, tapering off toward the side seams, below the armhole.

Bust and waistline

*The bodice front should hang straight from the shoulders now, and is ready to be fitted into the waist.
Pin off the ease and fullness into the side seams, beginning

at the underarm edge. The bodice muslin should now fit comfortably but not loosely over the bust.
The fullness below the bust should fall straight toward the waistline.
Pin off the side seam into the waist without causing the fullness under the bust to be pulled sideways.
Then, starting at the waist and using the pleat marks as your guide, pin this fullness into darts which should finish at the point of the bust.
Lengthen the pleat marks in the back section into darts also.

9. Problem Full bust.
Usually shown by drag lines from the bust toward the side seams at the waistline.
Correction Pin a tape in a straight line across the front of the muslin, starting and ending at the seamline on the lower grain line. Allow the grain line, but not the tape, to rise

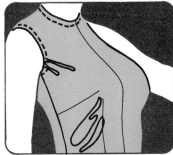

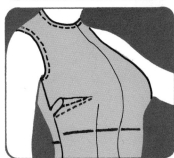

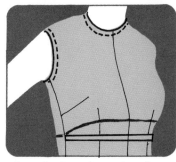

when the bust has taken it up.
Mark the muslin along the edge of the tape, using a different

colored pencil so that you cannot confuse this line with the grain line.
Remove the tape.
Undo the side seams and lift the fabric into the side bust dart on the lower stitching line only.
Check the crosswise grain line on the lower half of the muslin and don't pin any more into the side dart than will allow the grain line to run straight across the pattern.
The side seams will now be shorter, so pin a new line for the waist.

10. Problem Side bust darts in wrong position. The dart should run toward the point of the bust.

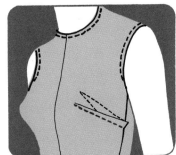

Correction If it is too high or too low, drop it or raise it.

11. Problem Shallow bust.
The point of the side bust dart creates fullness over the bust and does not run out smoothly. You will notice that the lower grain line curves downward toward the center front.

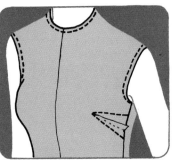

Correction Undo the side seams and let out the side bust dart on the lower stitching line, allowing the fabric to drop into the waist until the grain line runs straight across the pattern.
Repin the side seams, taking in the surplus width from the front.
Your armhole may need reshaping around the front.

12. Problem Underarm bulge.
Pulling under the armhole.

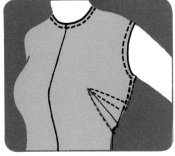

Correction Slant the side bust darts by making them a little lower at the side seams. Let out the side seams between the underarm dart and the armhole line.

*# Finishing the muslin
The grain lines should now be perfectly vertical and horizontal and the bodice should fit your figure well.
Finally, lay a narrow seam tape around your waist and pin it to the muslin. Mark in your correct waistline if it has altered.

319

Collector's Piece

The Age of Treasured Books

Throughout Tudor times, the covers of precious manuscripts and treasured religious books, usually the Bible, were enriched by embroidery and beadwork. This charming custom had, alas, come to an end by the time Charles II came to the throne in 1661, but many beautiful examples of early embroidered bookcovers still survive.

Although the original rich colorings are now somewhat faded, the striking designs in colored silks and gold and silver gilt threads

Later, velvet was used and beautiful effects were achieved with decorative embroidery contrasting with the texture of the velvet, together with a great deal of laid and couched work in gold thread.

As the craft developed, silk was used, usually white, allowing much finer work. Thick raised gilt borders protected the surface of the silk and embroidery and bags or satchels were provided for greater protection.

The bags were as carefully and lovingly worked as the bookcovers themselves, usually in silver thread on canvas, but were more durable. Some of the bags carried tassels on drawcord and silken carrying cords.

The books illustrated are in the Bodleian Library, Oxford, England and include all the types of book covers which are mentioned here.

still have much of their original beauty. One of the most exquisite examples, dating from the reign of Elizabeth I, is a Bible, made by a famous printer, Charles Barker, as his New Year present to the Queen in 1584. In crimson velvet, decorated with seed pearls and gold thread embroidery, the design incorporates the Royal insignia, bordered by a symmetrical arrangement of stems and flowers. Professional embroidery of this kind would probably have been done by men.

Three types of fabric were used for book and manuscript covers, the texture of the fabric dictating the design and the embroidery stitches. Early covers were made of canvas, the entire surface of the fabric being covered with tent-stitched designs. Queen Elizabeth, when still a small child, embroidered two canvas covers, one of which she gave to her mother, Ann Boleyn.

Party time for Sasha

In this chapter young readers and young-at-heart readers have a chance to add to the doll's wardrobe which began in Part 14, page 262. Although the party dress and coat in the directions were made for Sasha, they will fit any of your favorites who are about sixteen inches tall.
The pattern is basically a simple lace stitch and includes increasing, decreasing, working the eyelet rows for inserting the ribbon, and making buttonholes.

Gauge
7½sts and 10 rows to 1in over pattern worked on No.3 needles

Materials

4 ounces Sports Yarn
One pair No.3 needles (or Canadian No.10)
Two buttons
One yard narrow ribbon
Narrow lace for trimming, if desired

Party dress

Beginning at lower edge, cast on 103sts.
K 4 rows.
Continue in lace pattern:
1st row K.
2nd row P.
3rd row P1, *P2 tog, yrn, P1, yrn, P2 tog, P1, rep from * to end.
4th row P.
These 4 rows form the pattern.
Rep 1st-4th rows 10 times more.
K 1 row. P 1 row.
Next row K1, *K2 tog, K1,
322

rep from * to end. 69sts.
K 1 row.

Eyelet row
K1, *ytf, K2 tog, rep from * to end.
K 1 row.

Divide for armholes
1st row K15, bind off 6sts, K27, bind off 6sts, K15.
Complete left back first on last group of sts.
K 18 rows.

Shape neck
1st row Bind off 7sts, K8.
K 4 rows.

Shape shoulder
Next row Bind off 4sts, K to end.
K 1 row. Bind off rem 4sts.
With WS of work facing, rejoin yarn to center group of sts for front.
K 17 rows.

Shape neck and shoulders
1st row K8, bind off 11sts, K8.
** K 6 rows on 8sts.
8th row Bind off 4sts, K to end. K 1 row.
Bind off rem 4sts. **
With WS facing, rejoin yarn to rem 8sts, work to end of row.
Complete as for other shoulder, working from ** to **.
With WS of work facing, rejoin yarn to rem group of sts and K to end of row.
K 18 rows.
Next row Bind off 7sts, K to end.
K 4 rows on 8sts.

Shape shoulders
Next row Bind off 4sts, K to end.
K 1 row. Bind off rem 4sts.

Coat

Using No.3 needles, cast on 121sts.
K 4 rows.
Continue in pattern:
1st row K.
2nd row K3, P to last 3sts, K3.
3rd row K3, P1, *P2 tog, yrn, P1, yrn, P2 tog, P1, rep from * to last 3sts, K3.
4th row As 2nd.
Rep last 4 rows 10 times more, then 1st and 2nd rows once.
Next row K4, *K2 tog, K1, rep from * to last 3sts, K3. 83sts.
K 1 row.

Eyelet and buttonhole row
K1, ytf, K2 tog, K1, *ytf, K2 tog, rep from * to last 3sts, K3.
K 1 row.

Divide for armholes
1st row K18, bind off 8sts, K31, bind off 8sts, K18.
Complete left front on last group of sts.
K 1 row.
Next row K to last 5sts, K2 tog, K3.
Rep last 2 rows until 8sts rem.
K 3 rows.

Shape shoulder
Next row Bind off 4sts, K to end.
K 1 row. Bind off rem 4sts.
With WS of work facing, rejoin yarn to center group of sts, K to end of row.
K 20 rows.

Shape neck and shoulders
1st row K8, bind off 15sts, K8.
** K 2 rows on 8sts.

Shape shoulder
Next row Bind off 4sts, K4.
K 1 row. Bind off rem 4sts. **
With WS of work facing, rejoin

yarn to rem sts, K to end of row. Work as for other shoulder from ** to **.
With WS of work facing, rejoin yarn to rem sts and K to end of row.
Next row K3, sl 1, K1, psso, K to end.
K 1 row.
Rep last 2 rows until 8sts rem.
K 3 rows.

Shape shoulder
1st row Bind off 4sts, K4.
K 1 row. Bind off rem 4sts.

Sleeves

Using No.3 needles, cast on 31sts.
K 4 rows.
Work the 4 row pattern as given for party dress.
Work 32 rows.

Shape cap
Keeping pattern correct throughout, bind off 4sts at beg of next 2 rows.
Dec one st at each end of next and every RS row until 9sts rem.
Bind off rem sts.

Finishing

Darn all ends into edges of work.
Press each piece very lightly under a damp cloth with a warm iron.

Party dress
Sew shoulder seams.
Seam skirt to ½in below eyelet. Thread ribbon through eyelet row and sew on WS to secure ends.
Edge neck and armholes with narrow lace.
Make a button loop at top corner of back opening. Sew on button to correspond with button loop.

Coat
Sew shoulder and sleeve seams.
Sew in sleeves. Thread ribbon through eyelet row and sew ends on WS. Sew narrow lace around edges. Sew button on front edge to correspond with button loop.

It's party time for Sasha ▶

Snowsuits with a touch of Fair Isle

Make a snug snowsuit for a boy or a girl! Patterns for the matching mittens and cap will be in Part 18, page 344. Note: Be sure to buy all the yarn you'll need at one time.

Sizes

Directions are for size 6.
The figures in brackets [] refer to sizes 8, 10 and 12.
Jacket:
Sleeve seam, 10[11:12½:13½]in.
Length from edge to shoulder, 14½[16:18:19½]in.
Leggings:
Front seam, 9[9½:9½:9½]in.
Leg seam, 13½[16½:19½:22½]in.

> **Gauge**
> 5½sts and 7½ rows to 1in over stockinette stitch worked on No.5 needles

Materials

Knitting Worsted, 4oz balls
Jacket: 3[4:5:5] balls in main color A
1 ball each in contrast colors B, C and D
14[16:18:20]in open-end zipper
Leggings: 3[4:5:5] balls in main color A
Elastic for waist and feet
Mittens: 1 ball in color A
Small amounts of B, C and D
Cap: 2 balls in color A
1 ball each in B, C and D
One pair No.5 needles (or Canadian No.8)
One pair No.3 needles (or Canadian No.10)
Stitch holder

Jacket back

Using No.3 needles and A, cast on 68[72:80:84] sts.
1st row K3, *P2, K2, rep from * to last st, K1.

2nd row K1, *P2, K2, rep from * to last 3sts, P2, K1.
Rep 1st and 2nd rows 6[7:6:8] times more, then 1st row once.
Next row Rib 12[7:13:9] sts, (inc in next st, rib 20[13:25:15] sts) 2[4:2:4] times, inc in next st, rib to end.
71[77:83:89] sts.
Change to No.5 needles.
Beg with a K row, continue in st st until 9½[10½:12:13]in, or desired length, from beg, ending with a P row.

Shape armholes

Bind off 3sts at beg of next 2 rows.
Dec one st at each end of next and every other row until 51[55:59:63] sts rem.
Continue without shaping until work measures 14½[16:18:19½]in from beg, ending with a P row.

Shape shoulders

Bind off 5[5:6:6] sts at beg of next 4 rows, then 5[6:5:6] sts at beg of next 2 rows.
Slip rem 21[23:25:27] sts on holder.

Right front

Using No.3 needles and A, cast on 32[36:36:40] sts.
Work 15[18:15:19] rows rib as given for back.
Sizes 6, 10 and 12 only:
Next row (Rib 10[6:9] sts, inc in next st) 1[3:2] times, rib to end. 33[36:39:42] sts.
Change to No.5 needles.
Next row Bind off 12sts, K to end. 21[24:27:30] sts.
Beg with a P row, continue in st st until work measures same as back to underarm, ending at side edge.

Shape armhole

Bind off 3sts at beg of next row. Dec one st at armhole edge on next and every other row until 11[13:15:17] sts rem.
Continue without shaping until work measures same as back to shoulder, ending at armhole edge.

Shape shoulder

Sizes 6 and 8 only:
Bind off 5[6] sts at beg of next row. Work 1 row.
Bind off.

Sizes 10 and 12 only:
Bind off 5[5] sts at beg of next row and 5[6] sts at beg of following alt row. Work 1 row.
Bind off.

Left front

Using No.3 needles and A, cast on 32[36:36:40] sts.
Work 15[18:15:19] rows rib as given for back.
Sizes 6, 10 and 12 only:
Next row Rib 21[15:20] sts, (inc in next st, rib 10[6:9] sts) 1[3:2] times.
33[36:39:42] sts.
Change to No.5 needles and K to last 12sts, bind off 12sts.
Break off yarn and rejoin to rem sts. Complete as given for right front, reversing shapings.

Fair Isle bands

Using No.3 needles and A, with RS of right front facing, pick up and K 89[97:113:121] sts along front edge.
Next row P.
Change to No.5 needles.
Working rows 1-12 from chart, keeping odd rows in K and even rows in P and working the odd st as indicated at end of K rows and beg of P rows, work 3[3:1:1] rows from chart.

Shape neck

Bind off 8[8:11:11] sts at beg of next row. Dec one st at neck edge on every other row until 78[86:98:106] sts rem, ending with a WS row.
Work last 2 rows from chart.
Break off contrasts B, C and D.
Change to No.3 needles.
K 1 row.

Work 2 rows of P1, K1 rib.
Bind off tightly in rib.
Using No.3 needles and A, with RS of left front facing, pick up and K 89[97:113:121] sts along front edge.
Next row P.
Change to No.5 needles and work rows 1-12 from chart, shaping neck as follows:
Work 4[4:2:2] rows from chart.
Bind off 8[8:11:11] sts at beg of next row. Dec one st at neck edge on next and every other row until 78[86:98:106] sts rem.
Work last 2 rows from chart.
Break off contrasts B, C and D.
Change to No.3 needles.
K 1 row.
Work 2 rows of K1, P1 rib.
Bind off tightly in rib.

Sleeves

Using No.3 needles and A, cast on 32[36:36:40] sts.
Work 15[17:15:19] rows rib as given for back.
Next row Work in rib, inc 4[2:4:2] sts evenly across row.
36[38:40:42] sts.
Change to No.5 needles.
Beg with a K row, continue in st st, inc one st at each end of 3rd [3rd:5th:3rd] and every following 7th row until there are 52[56:60:64] sts.
Continue without shaping until work measures 10[11:12½:13½]in, or desired length, ending with a P row.

Shape cap

Bind off 3sts at beg of next 2 rows.
Dec one st at each end of next and every other row until 32[34:36:38] sts rem.
Bind off 3sts at beg of next 6[6:8:8] rows.
Bind off rem sts.

Neck border

Sew shoulder seams.
Using No.3 needles and A, with RS facing, pick up and K 23[24:26:27] sts up right side of neck, K across sts on holder for back inc 5[5:7:7] sts evenly and pick up and K 23[24:26:27] sts down left side of neck.

72[76:84:88] sts.
Beg with a 2nd row, work
2½[3½:4½:5½]in rib as given
for back.
Bind off in rib.

Leggings (right leg)

Using No.3 needles and A,
cast on 44[48:52:56] sts.
Work 10 rows rib as given for
jacket back, inc 4sts evenly
on last row.
48 [52:56:60] sts.
Change to No.5 needles.
1st row K.
2nd row P 11[12:13:14] sts,
sl 1P, P 24[26:28:30] sts,
sl 1P, P 11[12:13:14] sts.
Keeping sl st correct, work
2 rows more.
Next row Inc in first st,
K 22[24:26:28], M1K, K2,
M1K, K to last st, inc in last st.
Work 8[9:11:12] rows.
Next row Inc in first st,
work 24[26:28:30], M1K,
work 2, M1K, work to last st,
inc in last st.
Continue inc in this way on
every following 9th [10th:
12th:13th] row until there are
84[92:96:104] sts.
Continue without shaping
until work measures 12¾
[16:18¾:22]in from beg,
ending with a P row.
Inc one st at each end of next
and following 2[1:2:1] rows.
90[96:102:108] sts. Work 1
row.

Warm set for winter days ►

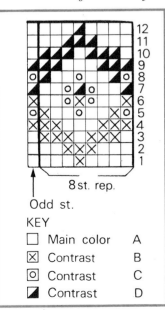

8 st. rep.

Odd st.

KEY
☐	Main color	A
☒	Contrast	B
⊙	Contrast	C
◤	Contrast	D

Fair Isle chart

Shape front and back edges
Bind off 2sts at beg of next
2 rows.
Dec one st at each end of 3rd
and every following 4th row
until 68[74:78:82] sts rem. **
Continue without shaping
until work measures 8[8:8½:
8½]in from bound-off sts,
ending with a K row.

Shape back
1st row P 48[48:60:60] sts.
Turn.
2nd and every other row K.
3rd row P 40[40:50:50] sts.
Turn.
5th row P 32[32:40:40] sts.
Turn.
Continue in this way until
P 8[8:10:10] and turn row

has been worked.
Next row K.
Next row P across all sts.
Change to No.3 needles.
Work 1 row of K1, P1 rib.
Bind off in rib.

Left leg

Work as for right leg to **.
Continue without shaping until
work measures 8[8:8½:8½]in
from bound-off sts, ending
with a P row.

Shape back
1st row K 48[48:60:60] sts.
Turn.
2nd and every other row P.
Complete as given for right
leg, reversing back shaping.

Finishing

Press each piece under a damp
cloth using a warm iron.

Jacket
Sew ends of front borders to
bound-off edge of ribbing. Sew
side and sleeve seams and
set in sleeves. Fold neckband
in half to WS and sl st in place.
Sew in zipper. Press seams.

Leggings
Fold legs at sl st and press
creases. Join front, back and
leg seams. Make casing stitch
at waist, insert elastic and join
ends. Sew elastic at each side
of leg at ankles to go under
foot. Press seams.

Narcissi and daisies

Easy-to-crochet flower motifs, edgings and braid are useful for decorating place mats and napkins. Make the mats from a crisp material such as linen, which is colorfast and easily laundered, or just stitch the crochet onto ready-made mats.

Materials

The illustrations show the crochet worked in Clark's Big Ball Mercerized crochet No. 30 using a No. B (2.00 mm) crochet hook. The choice of yarn depends entirely on whether you want a delicate finish or a thicker, more bulky appearance. For a bulky look, use Coats & Clark's O.N.T. Speed Cro-Sheen and a No. C (2.50 mm) crochet hook.

Prepare the mats and napkins in the size you want and work a narrow hem around all edges by hand or machine.

White narcissi on red linen

Double narcissus

1st round. Using yellow, ch5. Join to form a circle with a ss into first ch.

2nd round. Ch2, work 7sc into circle. Join with a ss into 2nd of first 2ch.

3rd round. Ch2, 1sc into front loop of each sc in previous round. Join with a ss into 2nd of first 2ch.

4th round. Ch2, 1sc into each sc of previous round, working through both strands at top of each stitch in the normal way. Join with a ss into 2nd of first 2ch.

5th round. As 4th. Break yarn and fasten off.

This forms a small ball for flower center.

6th round. Using white, place hook between one sc and the next of previous round, join with a ss, ch6, skip 2sc, *1sc between next 2sc, ch4, skip 2sc, rep from * once. Join with a ss into 2nd of first 6ch. This forms 3 loops.

7th round. Into each loop work 1sc, 1hdc, 3dc, 1hdc, 1sc. Join with a ss into first sc.

8th round. *Ch6, 1sc into 2nd dc of previous round, ch6, 1sc between sc where petals join, rep from * twice. Join with a ss into first of first 6ch. This forms 6 loops.

9th round. Into each loop of previous round work 1sc, 1hdc, 4dc, 1hdc, 1sc. Join with a ss into first sc. Break yarn and finish off. Work as many more flowers as you desire to fit around the edge of the mat. Sew firmly in place with thread.

Single narcissus

Work as given for double narcissus, finishing after the 7th round. Arrange in small groups and sew in place.

Braid

*Ch2, 1sc into first of 2ch, rep from * until the desired length. Pin around the mat from narcissus to narcissus and then sew securely with thread.

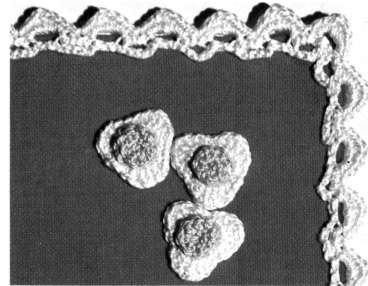

Detail of the single narcissus and edging

Detail of the double narcissus, edging and braid

Edging

Ch6. Work 1dc into first of 6ch thus forming a half loop, *ch5, turn work so that curve of next loop lies to the opposite side of the work from last loop and work 1dc into top of previous dc, rep from * until edging is the desired length. Work 2nd row along the length you have already worked, working into loops on one side only as follows: into ch5 loop work 3sc, 1hdc, 3sc, insert hook under next dc to left, work 1sc, rep along edging. Fasten off. Sew edging along hem of mat.

Finish napkins in same way.

White daisies on blue linen

N.B. To work a double treble (dtr), see the directions in Crochet Know-how chapter 3, page 46.

Daisy

1st round. Using yellow, ch6. Join to form a circle with a ss into first ch.

2nd round. Ch2, 11sc into circle. Join with a ss into 2nd of first 2ch.

3rd round. Ch4, 1ss into same st to form picot, *skip 1sc, 1sc into next sc, ch2, 1ss into same sc, rep from * 4 times. Break yarn and fasten off.

▲ *Red linen mat and napkin set showing narcissus motifs*

▼ *Cluster of daisies with lace ring edging and braid on a blue mat*

4th round. Using white, *insert hook from wrong side into skipped sc of previous round and join with a ss, ch5, into same st work 4dtr leaving last loop of each dtr on hook (5 loops on hook), yoh and draw through all loops, ch5, 1sc into same st to complete first petal, rep from * until 6 petals have been worked. Finish off. Work desired number of flowers and sew in place on linen.

Braid
Work as given for red set, twisting into loops as desired.

Lace ring edging
Each ring is formed and one side worked before making the next ring. After the desired length has been made, the second side of each ring is completed.

1st row. *Ch10, remove hook from last ch and insert into first ch, draw loop of last ch through the first to form a ring, work 6sc along one half of ring, rep from * until edging is the desired length.

2nd row. *Work 6 more sc into this ring, 1ss into last sc of previous ring, rep from * until each ring has been completed. Finish off and sew around edge.

When sewing on flowers and edgings, be careful that they are securely attached to the fabric, so that laundering is easy.

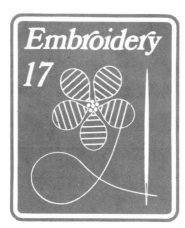

Designing for appliqué

It is very surprising how many people become really expert at embroidering commercial patterns who would never dream of attempting to create a design of their own. Designing for appliqué need not be difficult or complicated. In any case, bold, simple designs are often the most effective and you can always add to the interest and texture of the simplest design by your choice of embroidery stitches. Furthermore, if you try to do something so difficult that it is completely beyond you, you might easily be put off appliqué forever, whereas a successful first attempt will encourage you to go on to more intricate and exciting work.

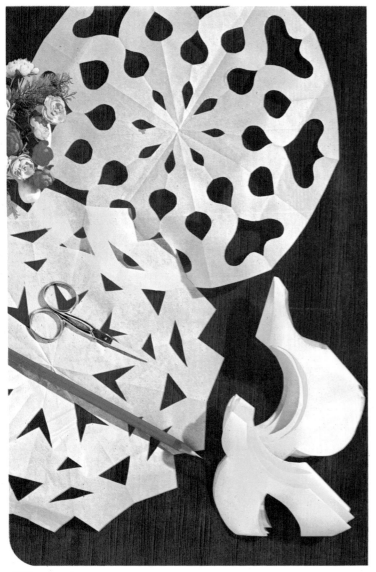

Creative appliqué

You do not have to be an artist to be able to design for embroidery, and appliqué is perhaps the easiest type to start on. The most important thing is to think in terms of large, simple shapes until you become more experienced. Small shapes are more difficult to handle, especially in materials which fray. Here are five easy ways to plan a design. And although they are for appliqué, they also apply to embroidery in general.

Folded and cut paper method

This is best used for non-fraying fabrics such as felt, suede, leather, synthetic leather, and plastic-coated materials. Fold a piece of paper twice diagonally to form a triangle and then twice more into smaller triangles. Cut out shapes (not too small), being careful not to cut away all the folded edges. Open out the paper and you have an instant design. Do not use the first one you make, but try several and choose the one you like best. Fold the paper in different ways to achieve different effects. A design formed in this way can then be applied to a contrasting color background so that it shows up through the cutouts. For a more advanced piece of work, apply two or more contrasting colors behind the cutouts.

Transfer or trace method

This is suitable for all types of embroidery and the sources of designs are endless. The illustrations to be found in modern children's books, magazines, wallpaper patterns and greeting cards all make interesting designs to be traced and transferred onto fabric.

Exploding a design

This method is again suitable for both embroidery and appliqué and results in asymmetric, abstract designs.

Start with a rectangle of paper—a color page from a glossy magazine is ideal because this will also help with choosing your color scheme. With a ruler and pencil, divide the paper into sections of varying shapes and sizes. Then clearly number each section so that you can keep the shapes in the same order when they are all cut out. Now cut along the drawn lines carefully and arrange the pieces in numerical order on a plain sheet of paper, spreading them out in a slightly haphazard manner until you are pleased with the pattern they form. Stick the shapes down with glue. Trace the design and transfer it to the fabric. This method can be used on folded circular pieces of paper, cutting random shapes right into the folds. These designs usually require the addition of decorative embroidery stitches.

Drawing around a shape

This method can be used where a single motif is desired, or to form all-over patterns using one or more motifs. Look around your home for items such as cookie cutters, ornaments with interestingly shaped bases, drinking glasses—in fact, anything which has an attractive but simple shape will do. Just draw around the base with a pencil and you have an instant design.

Designing with ready-made motifs

Felt motifs can be purchased at large stores. Use one on its own or group several to form quick, easy designs. Ribbons and braids are also exciting materials for appliqué designs as there are so many different ways you can use them. They can be found in glorious colors and varying widths—just right for creating lively designs either on their own or as part of a larger scheme. Braids are also useful for adding interesting textures to the over-all effect.

Designing symmetrical patterns by cutting out shapes from folded paper

The design traced or transferred onto both pieces of fabric

▲ *Cutting out the shape*   ▼ *The shape basted in place for surface stitching*

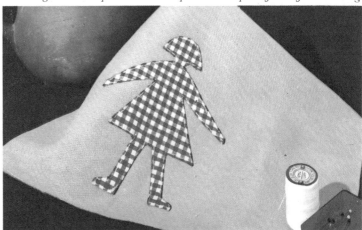

Appliqué step by step

1. Cut out the shapes used in the design in pieces of colored paper and place them in different positions on the background until you are satisfied with the color scheme and arrangement.
2. Transfer the outline of the design shapes onto the background fabric, using one of the methods described in Embroidery chapter 4, page 68.
3. Transfer the outline of shapes onto the fabric to be applied.
4. Use one of the basic methods of application described in Embroidery chapter 16, page 308.
5. Add further decoration, using hand or machine embroidery.

General hints

Whichever form of embroidery you prefer to use, it is important to be critical of your work. A good way in which to view this objectively is to hold it in front of a mirror. You will be amazed how different your work looks—in fact it will appear very much as others see it. If the design is tilting to one side, or is too far up or down on the background, the faults will show more clearly in the mirror reflection than when you look directly at it.

Blanket stitch or buttonhole stitch

This stitch, for which instructions are given in Embroidery chapter 10, is a good, strong stitch for sewing down applied shapes, either in its widely spaced form (blanket stitch) or in its closed-up form (buttonhole stitch). There are several variations, two of which are shown here. See Embroidery chapter 10 for others.

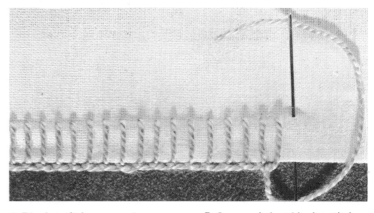

▲ *Blanket stitch*   ▼ *Long and short blanket stitch*

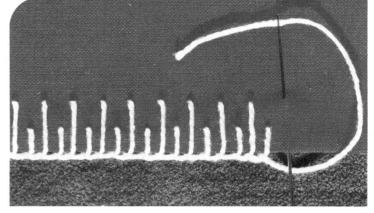

Fashion Flair

Add to dressmaking with knitting

Dressmakers: Team up with a friend who knits or pick up your own knitting needles and add knitted tops, sleeves or collars to your dressmaking or revamp last year's favorite dress. Or, knit a firm length of cloth on a knitting machine, place on your pattern pieces, machine stitch around the shapes, cut them out and proceed as for regular dressmaking. When stitching, baste $\frac{1}{4}$in tape to the seams when joining sections together.

Creative Hints on joining knitting to cloth: To put a roll collar and sleeves into a sleeveless dress, start by choosing a knitting pattern with sleeves and collar of a similar size to the openings in the dress. If you choose knitting and cloth of roughly the same weight, sew them together with an ordinary seam; otherwise, always stitch the knitting flat. If you find a knitted roll collar, armhole edge or cuff begins to stretch or pucker, run an elastic thread through the edge where it is joined to the woven fabric.

To avoid stretching when attaching a knitted top to a heavy fabric, make a chemise-type undergarment in lining fabric and join it where the knitting meets the fabric.

1. *Make a skirt and a rib-knit top and trim both with shiny vinyl or leather.*

2. *Cut off the top of an old dress which has a dated neckline, knit a short bodice and join the two together neatly.*

3. *Knit a long-length skinny top and add a skirt of lightweight printed wool.*

4. *This time, take sewing to knitting: Add a sewed lightweight wool tab fastening to a knitted or crocheted shirt. Wear with a crisp pleated skirt.*

5. *Add a ribbed collar and sleeves to a tweedy sleeveless dress. Ribbing's elasticity makes for neat sewing.*